TEACHER-CENTERED IN-SERVICE EDUCATION:

Planning and Products

by

Robert A. Luke

with the assistance of

ELLA HOLLY, MARIJA FUTCHS FINE, ANNA HYER

(Prepared under a grant from the
National Institute of Education)

NATIONAL EDUCATION ASSOCIATION
WASHINGTON, D.C.

Note

The opinions expressed in this publication should not be construed as representing the policy or position of the National Education Association. Materials published as part of the NEA Professional Studies series are intended to be discussion documents for teachers who are concerned with specialized interests of the profession.

Library of Congress Cataloging in Publication Data

Luke, Robert A.
    Teacher-centered in-service education.

    (Professional studies)
        1. Teachers—In-service training—United States.
I. National Education Association of the United States.
II. Title.   III. Series.
LB1731.L84   371.1'46   80-11729
ISBN 0-8106-1624-6

CONTENTS

LIST OF FIGURES, EXAMPLES, AND CHARTS

THE NEA STUDY OF IN-SERVICE EDUCATION

In 1975 the National Education Association received funds from the National Institute of Education to undertake a study of some aspects of teacher in-service education.

The NEA's In-Service Education Project was one of seven NIE-supported programs established to explore ways to close the gap between educational theory and practice. The NEA project, the only one of the seven to address the in-service education of teachers, extended over a three-year period ending June 30, 1979. The NEA was the only teachers association acting as a principal contractor.

All seven programs sought to learn how research-based and field-tested materials could be delivered to teachers; and to discover what teachers were able to do with such materials. These Research Development and Utilization Projects were all action/research programs.

The NEA project described and distributed information on about 600 in-service programs in the areas of the basic skills, career education, and teaching strategies. Cooperating states included Alabama, California, Iowa, Massachusetts, Michigan, Minnesota, Ohio, Pennsylvania, Tennessee, Washington, Wisconsin, and Wyoming. In each state the project had available the part-time services of two facilitators, one representing the state teachers association and the other the state department of education. Within these pilot states, fifty-seven local school districts participated as sites where project hypotheses were tested.

This book is written for teachers and others who design teacher-center and professional-development activities. Its purpose is to share the project's discoveries about the resources that enable teachers to learn *what* they want to learn about the art and science of teaching in the *ways* they want to learn.

Project staff completed the writing before the termination of the project. Publication costs, however, were not borne by the project. The book does not necessarily reflect the position or policies of the NIE and no official endorsement by NIE should be inferred. The project's work was performed under the terms and conditions of NIE contract number 400-76-0091.

ACKNOWLEDGMENTS

TEACHER-CENTERED IN-SERVICE EDUCATION: PLANNING AND PRO-DUCTS reflects the experience of many individuals who, over the past six years, have been engaged in two NEA-sponsored programs. Both programs examined methods of translating the much-repeated phrase "teacher involvement" from a slogan into effective ways of learning new skills and acquiring new understanding about teaching.

The real authors are teachers across the country who, with administrative and supervisory personnel, spent many hours as participants in in-service programs set up to test various hypotheses. Many of these participants assisted directly by providing information in data collection interviews and by maintaining activity logs. Special thanks are due the state facilitators in the twelve projects. A list of these individuals appears in the Appendix.

Nancy Eberhart, Director of the Division of Educational Redesign and Renewal, Ohio Department of Public Instruction, was instrumental in introducing the concept of individualizing in-service education into the project design and advised the author on the writing of the chapter directed to this subject.

Richard L. Sweeney, Director of Instruction and Professional Development for the Iowa State Education Association, actively participated in both the Teacher-Centered Professional Development (TCPD) program and the NIE-funded project. His *How Teachers Learn* exercise, included in the text, was developed for the TCPD program and was used again in training programs for state staff during the NEA In-service Education Project.

John Waters, Assistant Director of the ERIC Clearinghouse on Teacher Education, read chapter 9 and made necessary technical corrections.

Ruth Emory and Rene Pino of the Northwest Regional Educational Laboratory generously conferred with the author for a half-day. Many of their useful suggestions, particularly on training design, are now a part of this book.

Grateful appreciation is expressed to all who helped, especially the project staff, members of the NEA IPD staff, and colleagues who read and critiqued the manuscript.

CHAPTER 1

TEACHER-CENTERED IN-SERVICE EDUCATION

A great many teachers express dissatisfaction with the quantity and quality of in-service education available to them. The emphasis of this book is on a way to meet teacher in-service needs more adequately. It explores a range of new resources to help and spells out process steps for planning and program delivery that can be followed to good advantage in any in-service education setting where teacher-centering is a bias.

THE CONCEPT

The concept of in-service education for continued professional development, or as an extension of pre-service teacher training, embraces a host of complex and overlapping ideas.

"In-service" refers to learning that takes place after formal, undergraduate teacher preparation has been completed. In-service can also be interpreted to mean "learning-on-the-job," or "learning-while-earning." It can take place in a teacher center, in a school's general purpose room, in the classroom, or at a location entirely away from the school.

"Education" is generally thought to mean a teacher/student interaction in which a change in behavior, attitude, or skill is the desired outcome.

In human terms, "development" implies growth. Development may come about as much from maturation as from an organized educational program.

Equally complex are the concepts packed within "learning," "training," "professional," and other words which define the continuing education of teachers. Much has been theorized about the ways in which one concept interacts with other, similar concepts.

The issue of definition is raised to note that the subject dealt with by this book is a developing one, as yet incompletely understood. The whys and wherefores of in-service education are capable of providing intellectual grist for countless debates, national meetings, fact-finding commissions, and other forms of professional discussion. The subject increasingly pokes its controversial head into negotiation sessions between representatives of school trustees and teachers.

Nevertheless, in-service education does take place. Teachers and administrators are planning it, participating in it, evaluating it, and changing it.

Because this book deals with in-service education for *teachers* does not imply that learning more about teaching—and learning more about learning—is not a responsibility of all educators. Attention is focused on teachers because they comprise nearly sixty percent of the school staff. Of all educational staff, teachers are most visible to the community. They maintain closest contact with students. In that capacity, teachers have the greatest responsibility for what students learn in the classroom.

TEACHER-CENTERING AS A BIAS

The book has its own set of biases. One is that the most effective learning takes place when the learner has a hand in determining what he or she needs and wants to learn. The book also speaks to the point that teachers, like their students, learn in different ways. Styles of learning—and strategies of teaching—must be given the same careful consideration when the in-service program is planned as when instructional programs for children are developed.

The book strongly reflects the bias that, if in-service education is to overcome its deficiencies, it must focus on the strategies teachers can use to solve the problems they face in the classroom. The help teachers receive cannot be isolated from the laboratories of their own classrooms. Effective on-the-job learning cannot be relegated to weekends, after-school hours, or summer institutes. However, since in reality much training does take place at such times, this book cannot ignore these conditions in its planning suggestions.

It is important that teachers and administrators work together in planning the in-service program. To ensure such interaction, a policy board composed of teachers and administrators is a legal requirement of the federally funded teacher centers. The success of this jointly constituted group, and others like it, depends on good will—and on a clear notion of what the tasks are and how to implement them. An analysis of the winning ingredients of cooperative program planning represents an important part of this work.

In no way does the book profess to cover all aspects of in-service education. That it does not, for example, discuss the professional development programs offered by institutions of higher education, usually leading to advanced degrees, does not negate their crucial importance. That it does not treat the obligation of the board of education and the school administration to fulfill institutional mandates through in-service education does not imply that no such need exists.

The focus is on the aspect of in-service education that relates to serving goals teachers say are important to them and identifying new resources for meeting such goals. Whether they are best met in a workshop, a class, a course, or an institute is not discussed. Neither are any judgments made on offering in-service education for credit or noncredit, or voluntarily or compulsorily. The frequent use of the word "need" does not imply that in-service education is merely remedial. The "need" expressed by many teachers is to keep up to date, to add to or sharpen an established array of teaching strategies, and to find an organized way of learning from—and sharing with—their colleagues.

This book does not, however, focus on helping an individual instructor plan a course offering. It concentrates on involving small, related faculty groups, through committee representation, in planning learning experiences that deal as realistically as possible with specific classroom problems. This is an activity far removed from the traditional, and fast-fading, "in-service day" where a system's total faculty is brought together in the auditorium of the largest high school.

In virtually every school district this modern alternative can take place for at least some of the teachers during a part of each year. While not dependent upon specially developed in-service materials, on-the-job learning can be made easier by the increasing availability of validated products for in-service training. Sources and characteristics of these products are described in chapter 8.

This book has been designed to support cooperative planning. Using readily available training materials, teachers and administrators *can* cooperatively plan in-service programs that will meet teacher-expressed needs and that will be conducted in ways teachers say they like to learn. The book shares what has been learned from a variety of sources about participatory planning and encourages those who use it to adapt, augment, and abridge as each situation warrants.

CHAPTER 2

ORGANIZATION OF PLANNING COMMITTEES

CENTRAL PLANNING COMMITTEE

The committee structure established to plan an in-service education program will vary from district to district. It will differ according to the size of the district, the philosophic notions about in-service education, the available budget, and the past success of the local association in insuring meaningful teacher input. The structure suggested in this book is drawn from the successful, cumulative experience of many of the sites participating in the NEA study described earlier. It consists of one central, districtwide committee and a subcommittee for each separate in-service education program to be organized.

It is important, of course, that all committees at whatever level be jointly representative of teacher and administrative staff members. The exact proportion of membership is a matter influenced by federal or state law, negotiated contract limitation, mutually acceptable precedents, or local custom. The suggested committee structure is shown diagrammatically in Figure 1.

The central district committee sets policy, secures operating funds, selects client groups, monitors programs, consults with building-level committees, and otherwise provides direction for a professionl development program. In a federally funded teacher center this committee would be the policy board. In a teacher center operated by a university or school district,or under private auspices, a governing board would serve this purpose. In a local in-service education program it would be a joint, districtwide committee of teachers named by the officers of their local education association and administrative personnel named by the superintendent of schools. All three teaching levels—elementary, middle school, and secondary school—would be represented. The teachers' responsibility is to be spokespersons for teachers who need and want help in doing an effective job with their students in classrooms. The responsibility of the administratie and supervisory members of the central committee is to interpret and implement school board policy, to run interference when funds and personnel are required, and to provide a perspective on total school needs. The joint responsibility of both groups is to provide the leadership required for the planning and operation of a meaningful in-service education program.

AN ANALOGY

In some respects, planning an in-service education program, i.e., putting together a number of different learning experiences into a coherent, developmental pattern, is not too unlike the processes involved in planning to buy or trade an automobile.

Figure 1. In-Service Education Planning Structure

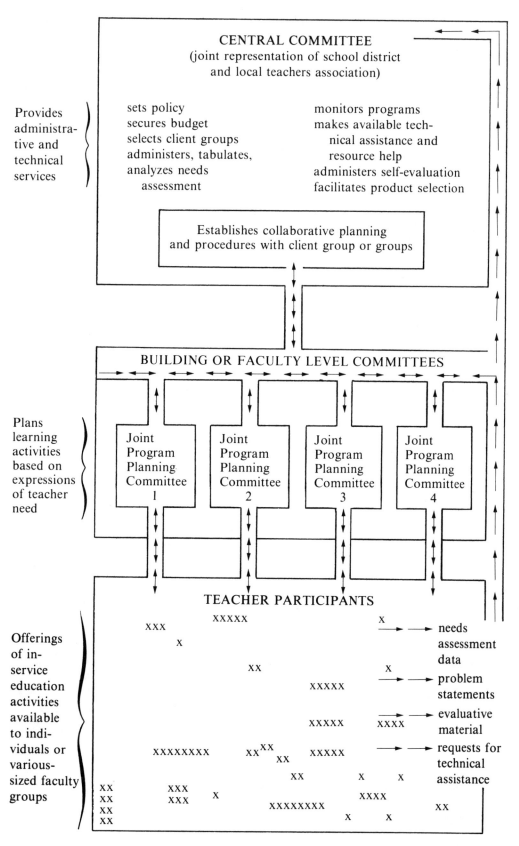

Before the crucial decision to buy or not to buy is reached, many preliminary steps must be taken. Need must be established, financing in sight, and time set aside for looking and thinking. Many hours are spent perusing newspaper columns, visiting showrooms, strolling through used car lots, and talking to friends. Then, the amount of budget available for purchase is considered and reconsidered. Even within this start limitation, however, options remain—all of which require careful decision making and frequent review. Are long-range goals best met by buying a new car or a "formerly owned" car? In view of gasoline conservation considerations, should some beloved luxury features of the old car be scrapped in favor of a simpler, but more practical, model? Even the number of available dollars can be manipulated. Shopping for the most favorable financing is always worthwhile—an alternative to consider is fixing up the old bus and making it do for a few more years.

The use of technical assistance is a necessity. Few families, no matter how talented, possess within one membership group all the skills and information required to make unadvised judgments about the alternative financing options usually available, the meaning of technical specifications, or an objective analysis of the potential mechanical longevity of the present car.

After purchase of the car, the experience of individuals more skilled in diagnosing mysterious squeaks and noises, care of upholstery, or adjustment of hidden parts is frequently a necessity. Such information can be delivered in many ways—by relying on the advice of the mechanics employed by the dealer, by carefully reading the owner's manual, by enrolling in an adult education class on automative tuneup, or by conning a knowledgeable colleague or neighbor into serving as consultant.

Although a now-that-it-is-all-over evaluation is always useful as a learning device—and helpful in making corrections—it is no substitute for first securing all the advice and expert consultation possible, carefully thinking through all alternatives, and deciding among them.

THE AGENDA FOR PLANNING

Translating the analogy into in-service education terms means that the structure for program planning can begin with aspirations and good intentions. From that point forward, each step requires detailed planning. For effective in-service education, planning takes time and costs money, and no single group of individuals can be assumed to know all there is to know about executing each step in the planning process.

To be effective, in-service education planning must be comprehensive. It must have a base in official school policy. It must have a planning structure which encompasses a central committee and subcommittees. It also requires a long-range projection of goals and objectives and a precise strategy for including in the in-service education program either all the teachers all the time or designated groups of teachers at designated times. Planning must be further extended to assure an adequate budget, time allocations, a needs assessment, the development of problem statements, and the identification of resource material and personnel. Even after all these provisions have been made, the formidable task of planning a series of learning experiences still lies ahead.

One of the recurring findings of the NEA project study was the relatively small amount of time spent by teachers serving on project committees in planning the installation and implementation of programs after selecting and receiving the training materials.

Long hours were spent designing a needs assessment and considering products to purchase. But once the materials were received, little time was directed to planning their use. In some cases the products were late in arriving or the directions for their use were so well spelled out that no step-by-step planning was required. Often the in-service education committee members had no experience in this kind of planning and awareness of the kinds of detailed, time-consuming activities required to offer teachers a program that was "practical," "down to earth," and "related to teacher needs."

Data uncovered by the project also clearly indicated that planning groups rarely found any need to call for help, i.e., technical assistance from individuals with planning expertise. This was true in spite of the fact that planning, like the ability to grow showcase roses, is more than a knack—it is a set of highly specialized skills—and like any skill calls for some background knowledge and practice opportunities. Chapter 4 describes methods of acquiring such skill.

SELECTION OF TRAINING GROUPS

The second rung of committee structure is made up of a separate buildingwide or faculty-cluster committee for each in-service education program designated in the operational plan for the current school year.

The identification of specific schools or faculty groups as recipients of an in-service program represents one of the most difficult decisions the central committee must make. Even in the most affluent districts, or in those with large teacher centers, it is usually impossible to assure all teachers that, whenever they like, they can be given adequate opportunity on school time and in a situation related to their own classrooms to learn more about teaching. An alternative, set forth in terms of a long-range plan, might, for example, be to direct available in-service education resources toward working with elementary school teachers one year, intermediate level teachers, the next year, and secondary school teachers, the following year. It might project working with all first grade and seventh grade teachers one year and then move up one grade level each following year. It could be a plan to work with subject areas in a designated sequence. Devising such a plan is a major responsibility of the central committee, which obviously must have access to long-range district planning data, in-depth understanding of needs assessment results, and a deep commitment to the give-and-take process and constant review implied by such a task.

Whatever target groups are identified, however, specific program planning must be decentralized to include representatives of the faculties of individual schools, departments, or grade levels. Direct representations of each of these groups of teachers on their own program planning committee is a basic requirement for effective program development.

BUILDING- OR FACULTY-LEVEL COMMITTEES

Imagine, if you will, a committee of perhaps a dozen individuals seated in a conference room around a table or in a well-equipped classroom with tables, chairs, and a great deal of chalkboard space.

The meeting is not organized around a brown bag luncheon. Nor is the group hurriedly convening after school or on a Saturday morning. The meeting may be any school day of the week and the committee members have time during the regular school day away from classroom duties to devote full attention to planning. To complete the process, the equivalent of three full days of planning time, however divided and distributed over as many weeks as required, will probably be necessary.

The committee will have among its membership one or more representatives from the districtwide central planning committee. More members, however, represent the clients served by the program.

One participant is present because of a special expertise in workshop planning. This individual's study of educational questions has led to a consideration at some point of how *adults* learn: how they learn as individuals, and how they learn in large and small group situations. This individual may be a teacher whose work outside the classroom, perhaps in the dispatch of association duties, has developed for her/him the reputation of an effective conference leader. It may be an assistant district superintendent who is known to be able to secure effective teacher involvement in curriculum planning, or a principal who works well with parents. In some school systems it may be a teacher from the adult education program, the director of the staff development program, or a consultant employed for this purpose and brought in from a nearby college, university, or local employee training program. State department of education personnel are often available to provide this kind of assistance.

And, most important, it might be you who, after studying the suggestions contained in this book, want to give it a go yourself.

This individual is present because the district's central planning committee has recognized the need for a *technical consultant:* someone whose major responsibility is not to advise on what is to be learned, but to be alert to the strategies employed in getting across to teachers what they say they want to learn. The other members of the committee—eleven in this illustration—are then free to concentrate on the learning needs identified by teachers and the content covered in films, taped lectures, or other substantive materials included in the products to be selected and used.

CRITERIA FOR COMMITTEE MEMBERSHIP

The teacher members of the committee may have volunteered for the assignment or may have been appointed by some arm of the local association. The principal criteria governing selection included teaching ability and participation in the needs assessment used to identify the problem area around which the in-service program is to be planned, as well as a perception by colleagues that the individual is generally representative of them. It is understood that needs assessment data are at hand. The committee member is not expected to know intuitively all the problems and concerns of each individual teacher he/she represents. With a technical consultant available, the member need not be an expert on how adults, i.e., teachers, learn. With a supply of validated in-service products to work from, the member need not be a subject matter expert. What each member of the committee must be, however, is a reliable spokesperson for the group he/she represents; an individual who is able to sense what his/her colleagues think, but who owes this sensitivity more to influences drawn from needs assessment or problem statement data than from his/her own speculations. The effective committee member is one who is willing to take the time to check back with colleagues for further guidance whenever the need arises.

The committee member should also represent her/himself: a good teacher who, from individual training and teaching experience, understands motivation, problem solving, and evaluation, and is familiar with the psychological blocks to, and supports for, the learning process. One who knows what good teaching is—who is her/himself a good teacher—will be an effective committee member when planning learning experiences for others. If the design emerging from the planning process suddenly seems overly formal or didactic; or appears to be meeting the needs of the planners more than the expressed needs of potential participants; or is crowding too much into an agreed-upon time frame, then the pedagogical instincts of the good teacher should be aroused and a call issued for a review of the plans.

Ideally, the committee chairperson is not selected solely because of high status as an administrator or a teacher-leader. The chairperson should possess the following abilities to keep a group moving, and to formulate an agenda combining a listing of obvious tasks with enough free play built in for working on the unanticipated needs and interests of others as they arise.

The heart of the action thus takes place at a point as close as possible to the faculty group to be served. Chapters 4, 5, and 6 describe how a joint committee of teachers and other school personnel, at a building- or faculty-interest level, can go about its planning tasks.

CHAPTER 3

TEACHER-CENTERED NEEDS ASSESSMENT

Teachers understand the importance of school officials making available in-service education activities that meet the system's instructional needs—legislatively mandated programs, the need to install new curricula, the decision to introduce an innovation in classroom organization, a new student evaluation system, or an upgrading of the skills of parent conferencing. All these and many other systemwide or grade-levelwide responses to student and community needs cannot be successful, however, unless accompanied by meaningful in-service education.

A basic requirement for the intelligent functioning of any school system is the need for an understanding on the part of the total staff of the characteristics of the student population. A systematic review of current data on student achievement, dropout rates and causes, the results of followup studies on graduates, and other relevant student-based information must be a part of every school's instructional development program.

Related to, yet different from, the "institutional" requirements for constantly updating the knowledge and skill level of the staff are the needs an individual teacher may feel can best be met by independent study, graduate work, or a travel-centered sabbatical. It may be the need to acquire another Romance language—or to qualify for an administrative postion—or to gain an advanced academic degree. If a sabbatical or other independent study program is not available, needs of this kind can be met by the teacher at personal convenience, on personal time, and at personal expense.

Falling between the training needs of the institution and the training needs of individual teachers are those instructional needs that confront members of a faculty; needs that could not possibly be foreseen nor adequately fulfilled in pre-service training—and often unlikely to be perceived by members of the school administration or board of education in the same way they are perceived by teachers. Such needs pertain to handling day-to-day problems of instruction, knowledge and availability of resource materials, organization and interrelationship of subject matter, and various problems in dealing with complicated student relationships or classroom communication processes.

Incentives to participate in this kind of in-service education are often limited to salary or degree increments. The training is usually a "class" composed of individuals from throughout the system—or beyond it. Because of the heterogeneous nature of those enrolled, the training necessarily requires a relatively high degree of abstraction to be applicable to all.

The first step in reducing the level of abstraction in the response to the instructional needs of a faculty group is to find a way to pinpoint needs. To achieve this aim, a systematic, personalized, well-thought-out data collection process is a must.

BASIC PRINCIPLES

Meaningful needs assessment does not have to be an overwhelming and complicated procedure. Often organized personal interviews, small group discussions, and not-too-complicated questionnaires will clearly elicit teacher concerns for the in-service assistance they require for the professional insights needed for day-to-day tasks. When a variety of inquiries can be combined and coordinated, the perception by the central planning committee of the needs of all teachers will be enhanced.

Two principles should be remembered if the needs assessment is to lead to effective plans for in-service education:

1. Teachers must be involved in *all* steps that are a part of the needs assessment process.

Sometimes teacher participation is limited to the opportunity to check a questionnaire or write in an additional response in the space provided. Full involvement implies participating in the planning process at the time the activity is first conceptualized, contributing to decisions on *how* the data are to be collected, and sharing in the final interpretation of the information supplied. In the model suggested in this book, full involvement is one of the responsibilities of the joint committee at the district level.

2. An intrinsic part of the needs assessment process is gathering data on the delivery system teachers perceive to be most effective in making available to them the skills and information they say they require.

All styles of learning cannot be accommodated in a single in-service activity, but most programs can be enhanced by the availability of a variety of teaching/learning modes. Encouraging the teacher to think creatively about individual learning patterns is a strong force against tolerating a conformity of learning in the in-service experience that would not be considered acceptable in the teacher's own classroom.

PUTTING PRINCIPLES INTO ACTION

In the implementation of these general principles, three steps should be followed prior to making the data available to the building-level or faculty group committees responsible for planning specific programs.

Step 1. Initial Planning. One of the earliest decisions to be made by the district joint committee is to identify the most useful way, or ways, of making an assessment of *teachers' needs*. Will the method use paper-and-pencil instruments, face-to-face needs assessment workshops, and evaluation of existing programs by individual interviews, informal conversations, or some combination of all these techniques?

Step 2. Collecting and Tabulating Data. Two approaches exist. The questionnaire, an easily administered and tabulated instrument for assessing in-service education needs, provides one vehicle for gathering the data required to plan the in-service program. If the survey is done on a building-by-building basis, it is relatively easy to tabulate the responses. It does not, however, provide a great deal of in-depth information and lacks the diagnostic dimension ("Why is it a problem? What evidence do you have?") that can be provided by a more interactive procedure.

When using a survey form it is also helpful to ask participants to provide information about themselves to better determine, for example, if middle school teachers on one side of town are making one kind of request and their counterparts across town another. Sometimes it is helpful to ask teachers to give their names on a questionnaire so that there can be direct followup to determine the exact nature of their in-service education needs. In other situations, the opportunity to remain anonymous may lead to more objective responses.

THE NEEDS ASSESSMENT WORKSHOP

Data for a needs assessment can also be generated in small interactive groups. One plan calls for the teachers in a given school, at the time of a regular faculty meeting or during the in-service days at the beginning of the school year, to talk for about two hours in small groups of five or six about their concerns and aspirations for meaningful in-service education. The questions posed must be precise and unambiguous—yet open-ended enough to permit considerable free discussion. For instance: "When you think about teaching your class tomorrow, what is the one most pressing concern or anxiety you have about doing the best possible job?" or "As you think about next month or next semester, what different or additional concerns do you think will then be uppermost in your mind?" and "Why do you name these problems and not some others?"

In small groups of coworkers—those who probably tend to talk occasionally about such things over lunch anyway—or over a bridge table—and with the assurance that a group report, not individual reports, will be made, it is often possible for individuals under a minimum of threat to "think aloud" among their peers about their reasons for a particular concern. Does it have something to do with the students? with the school system? with the parents? with themselves? Probably all play a part.

A second type of question that can be discussed in small group meetings is the teachers' preferred method of learning to be used in acquiring (or renewing) missing (or rusty) skills. For example: "What kinds of specific help would be most useful to you: seminars and workshops based on sound basic research, viewing films, conferences with other teachers, university or in-service classes, independent study, team visitation between schools, participation in organized research, volunteer work in the community?"

A related type of question might also be asked: "In what kind of setting do you think you do the best job of acquiring new teaching behaviors or learning new skills?" or "If you could participate in any kind of in-service activity you like, how would it be set up and administered?"

A suggested format for a needs assessment workshop of the kind described is given in Example 1.

THE THIRD STEP

Step 3. Analyzing Data. However the data are collected, whether by pencil-and-paper instruments or in small groups, they must be tabulated and analyzed. Whether machine tabulation is used or not, this should be done on a building-by-building and/or faculty group basis. In analyzing the meaning of the data, questions such as these might be asked: "In general, what do these responses indicate is needed?" (e.g., More opportunity to work with other teachers? Greater access to validated data and a wider variety of learning methodologies? Released time for independent study? Less in-service education that is unrelated to daily teaching requirements?), and "What specific in-service activities can be identified from the data as à means of helping teachers teach better?" (e.g., Opportunity to record teaching on videotape for reaction by another teacher and perhaps some students?).

REFERRAL TO BUILDING OR FACULTY GROUP COMMITTEES

Once all the data from a needs assessment, however secured, have been collected, tabulated, and analyzed, the most difficult job still lies ahead: using the data in such a way that programs are developed that will meet and fulfill teacher expectations. At this critical juncture, time, imagination, and expert consultative help are required.

Notwithstanding the importance of needs assessment, if its delivery falters, the whole operation will have been for naught. After the program is functioning, it must be monitored to assure that it meets quality standards. At its conclusion, the usefulness of the program must be evaluated; and eventually plans must be made for another year or another sequence of training. All of which comes back to the beginning of the cycle: the recognition that needs assessment, like learning itself, is a career-long, continuous process.

The preceding planning tasks must be undertaken by committees made up of teachers and others who are in regular communication with teachers who supplied the data. These tasks will be detailed in the chapters which follow.

Example 1. Leader's Guide

DESIGN FOR A
NEEDS ASSESSMENT WORKSHOP

TOPIC: What every teacher wants from in-service education—but hasn't yet had the chance to ask for.

First hour

Step 1.   Loosening up—getting reacquainted—forming heterogeneous work groups. Chairs prearranged in circles of six or eight.

Step 2.   Each circle selects a leader and recorder.

Step 3.   The workshop director assigns each circle the following tasks:

   a. Each person in the group (including the circle leader) talks briefly to others in the circle about his or her one, single greatest problem in the process of helping *students* learn. (Ruled out of order for this task are such considerations as too large a class, worry about meeting month-end bills, and other administrative or purely personal questions. The focus is on *teaching* skills: motivation, diagnosing learning difficulties, etc.)

   b. After each person in the circle has had an opportunity to state his or her concern, the circle leader asks each participant to state *why* he or she thinks it is a problem.

   c. As a third go-round, the circle leader asks each participant to try to identify the one skill or knowledge needed to help him/her do a better job in the particular problem area identified.

   d. Together, the members of the circle help their recorder fill out Report Form I (see Example 2).

Step 4.   The circle recorder or leader makes a brief report to the total workshop and hands in Report Form I.

Example 1. Leader's Guide *(continued)*

Second hour

Step 1.   The workshop director assigns each circle the following additional tasks:

   a. Each person in the circle is to think aloud about the best ways of *acquiring* for him/herself needed skills, knowledges, or information identified earlier.

   b. The circle members are encouraged to think imaginatively—to assume released time—to respond to the way he/she would learn best—not necessarily the easiest or least expensive way.

Step 2.   Members of the circle assist the recorder fill out Report Form II (see Example 3).

Step 3.   The circle or recorder leader reports to the total workshop on one "need" and the matching desired learning experience (method—form of delivery).

Step 4.   Reporters hand in Report Form II.

Step 5.   (Time permitting) As a total group, the workshop director introduces a discussion of the policy guidelines felt to best reflect the tone, spirit, or overall intent of the group's philosophy of meaningful in-service education.

Example 2. Needs Assessment Report Form I

What were the problems (needs) identified? No more can be listed than the number in the circle. Each participant reports only his or her most pressing instructional concern or anxiety, listing in "how-to" terms. If there is consensus on one or two, list only those.

      1.   How to . . .

      2.   How to . . .

      3.   How to . . .

      4.   How to . . .

      5.   How to . . .

      6.   How to . . .

List, in an order corresponding to the preceding section, the reason given for the existence of the particular problem.

      1.

      2.

      3

      4.

      5.

      6.

List, again in corresponding order, the skills or knowledges most needed to strengthen or improve skills or to otherwise overcome the problem area.

      1.

      2.

      3.

      4.

      5.

      6.

Example 3.   Needs Assessment Report Form II

Problem (Need)   *How Best Met*

1.   1.

2.   2.

3.   3.

4.   4.

5.   5.

6.   6.

CHAPTER 4

PLANNING SEQUENCE I: PLANNING AS LEARNING

As an organizational convenience the planning functions discussed in this book are divided into three large segments:

1. The initial meeting of planning committees (this chapter)
2. Writing a problem statement and identifying training materials (chapter 5)
3. Designing a training program (chapter 6).

When a new school is built the sensitive architect will want, and the enlightened school administration will insist upon, teacher input as a part of the planning process. The architect is interested not only in teacher ideas about a convenient floor plan or needed facilities, but also in discovering what kind of atmosphere the school should convey and what is needed to make it feel warm and inviting to students and faculty alike.

Somewhat similarly, the planning committee has an obligation to try to experience as best it can what it is like to participate in a creative, innovative in-service education activity. (Presumably most members will have had experience in what they consider nonproductive in-service education activities.) One way to achieve this is for planners of in-service education programs to participate themselves in the kinds of learning opportunities known to transform in-service education from a routine pouring in of information to the productive, active learning experience it can be.

The distribution of the agenda (or writing it on the chalkboard or on newsprint) can, in and of itself, provide a pretaste of the kind of imaginative, nontraditionbound planning expected of the committee. The proposed agenda for the initial committee meeting might read something like this:

1. What are my responsibilities?
2. What is our task? Planning for or planning with?
3. How do adults (i.e., teachers) learn?
4. Does motivation happen—or can it be planned?
5. Using this day's work as an example, what have we learned about teaching strategies?

CLARIFYING RESPONSIBILITIES OF PARTICIPANTS

The announced purpose of the first agenda item, "What are my responsibilities?" is, through discussion (perhaps generated by passing around a sheet of paper with this heading), for each participant to begin to think about her/his unique contributions to the total task. In more technical terms this might be called role identification or establishing role security. It also tends to help each member of the group begin to think about how she/he can contribute to the learning of others.

But why go through such an exercise?

There is ample evidence to support the theory that an individual's ability to learn is frequently lowered if too many questions remain unanswered for too long a time about her/his relationship to other learners. In in-service education terms this can be translated into concerns, even among those who teach together in the same school, as to whether or not an individual really belongs in a particular learning situation at a particular time. "Am I going to be shown up as the least informed member of the group?" "Is my experience such that I should be meeting with a more advanced group?" The opportunity for some exploration of these questions can usually be counted upon to increase what might be called "psychological comfort" by revealing that the backgrounds and experiences of each individual in the in-service education setting are such that everyone has something unique to contribute—and that everyone has something to learn.

Beginning the planning session in a similar way gives the members of the committee not only an opportunity to establish themselves in a new group but also to gain some insight into how new members of an in-service education activity may feel when taken out of the role of teacher and placed in the role of learner.

BEING CLEAR ABOUT THE TASK

The second agenda item is designed to focus on the tasks of the planning committee as the people in the middle: individuals who receive overall policy direction from the central committee but who, working from data supplied by teachers they represent at the building or departmental level, are responsible for fashioning learning activities for their peers. At this time they can face the question of the extent to which the administrative restrictions of time and money make it necessary for them to do all the planning for their colleagues and the extent to which they can check plans with their constituencies.

REVIEWING HOW ADULTS LEARN

The third agenda item for the first program planning segment would be introduced by the technical consultant or by any member of the committee who, using the material presented in this book as a guide, takes on the role of technical consultant. This item calls for the committee members themselves to take time for a bit of in-service education using the "How Teachers Learn" exercise. The step-wise procedure for conducting an exercise of this kind is described in Example 4. The purpose is to provide a setting in which the planning committee members can recall the kinds of learning experiences that were responsible for bringing about significant changes in behavior or viewpoint in their own lives.

Example 4. How Teachers Learn

Directions to the Leader:

Step 1. Announce the purpose of the exercise: to create a data bank of information and ideas about a delivery system for in-service education.

Step 2. a. Participants, working alone, are asked to spend a few minutes reflecting about two, three, or more experiences that have led to their better individual performance as teachers. Indicate that these experiences could have been as an individual or a part of a group; either while teaching or on some other job; in graduate school or outside school; formal or informal; paid for by someone else, by the individual, or the kind of experience where cost was not involved.

b. After some time has been provided for reflection, ask the group members to jot down some of these experiences on the Learning Inventory Form. (A training variation could be to pair participants and give each pair an opportunity to explore meaningful learning experiences with each other before writing them down.)

Step 3. In general group discussion participants spend the next half-hour on the following topic:

Based on the learning inventory we have just made, what kinds of experiences do teachers report as having been of most help in teaching them a new skill? in developing an "attitude"? in gaining a new insight? What are the implications of this information and those ideas for designing an in-service education program or for teacher-center planning? Use the "Idea Stockpiling" form (which follows) to organize the ideas.

Example 4. How Teachers Learn *(continued)*

LEARNING INVENTORY FORM

A. What professional experiences have made you a better teacher?

EXPERIENCE	IN/OUT SCHOOL	JOB-RELATED	CREDIT	EXPENSE
Examples:				
Counselor in a summer camp	out	no	no	paid job
In-service (metric)	in	yes	no	school
Group Process Training	out	no	no	mine
_____				
_____				
_____				
_____				
_____				

B. What activities in your life have you experienced that make you feel like a better person and a better teacher?

Examples: Membership in a book review club, educational study tour to Black Hills, volunteer work for a health agency.

_____

_____

_____

_____

_____

_____

Example 4. How Teachers Learn *(continued)*

STOCKPILING IDEAS ABOUT
EFFECTIVE IN-SERVICE EDUCATION METHODOLOGIES

In what type of activities would you like to be involved through a staff development program? (Ideas of *what has to happen* to assure a complete learning experience: plan and execute a microteaching exercise using other teachers as "students"; videotape a portion of your teaching day in your classroom; tape record a parent conference for later analysis with other teachers and/or parents. Be brief but provide enough detail to communicate your idea to others.)

1. _____
   _____
   _____
   _____

2. _____
   _____
   _____
   _____

3. _____
   _____
   _____
   _____

4. _____
   _____
   _____
   _____

5. _____
   _____
   _____
   _____

Example 4. How Teachers Learn *(continued)*

WHAT TURNS YOU ON
TO LEARN MORE ABOUT TEACHING—AND WHY

Part I

Rate in numerical order:

_____ Learning for learning's sake

_____ Upgrading my teaching certificate

_____ Gaining the approval of my peers

_____ Increasing my chance for promotion

_____ Gaining respite from classroom duties

_____ Finding intellectual stimulation and renewal

_____ Advancing my eligibility for a salary increase

_____ Understanding educational issues

_____ Learning new teaching skills

_____ Solving specific problems encountered in my teaching

_____ Earning graduate credit

_____ Making new friends

_____ Other (specify)_____

_____ Other (specify)_____

_____ Other (specify)_____

Part II

It is not necessary to write out "answers" to this question, but, now that you have completed the preceding checklist, go back and review in your own mind the reasons you checked the way you did. Why was the item you checked number one on your list? Why did some "reasons" have a low priority? What does this tell you about your own motivations?

THINKING ABOUT MOTIVATION

Related to an understanding of "how teachers learn" is the question of motivation. *Why do teachers want to learn?* The more closely an exploration of this question can be tied to a search by committee members of their own motivations, the more realistic the resulting insights will become. An exercise to stimulate this kind of examination is also outlined in Example 4. It asks committee members to rank numerically the incentives that would influence them to participate in a teacher center activity or other professional development program, and to reflect on the reasons behind their considered judgments.

It cannot be assumed that the motivations of the planning group to learn more about teaching will be the same as those of the client group. It can be predicted, however, that there will be considerable overlap. The relevant learning of the exercise will be found in a discussion of what an examination of an individual's own motivations reveals about the complexity of motivational forces in general. What does it take to initiate a decision to act? Once a decision is made, what direction will it take? To what extent is motivation an internal force? When, and under what circumstances, can it be influenced by outside forces?

Even a small exposure to some of the aspects of motivation as they relate to human behavior will reduce the number of simplistic assumptions about "how are we going to motivate other teachers?" that might otherwise creep into the sessions of the planning meeting.

PURPOSEFUL EVALUATION

The final agenda item of the planning component, "What have we learned about teaching strategies from today's planning meeting?" is designed to give the committee members an opportunity to review and reflect upon the various participative learning activities they shared during the day. The evaluative discussion might begin by a look at the question "Has the planning session itself reflected any of the common list of teacher complaints about many in-service education programs?" If there is consensus that parts of the committee's work are seen in retrospect as "dull," "boring," or "unnecessary busywork," the committee members need to reflect how, if they hope to plan a program that avoids these common pitfalls, they themselves can avoid them in their own meetings. Obviously the reverse is true: ways of learning or solving problems that worked for the planning committee can be predicted to work for other teachers.

The subheadings of this chapter are as follows:

Clarifying Responsibilities of Participants
Being Clear About the Task
Reviewing How Adults Learn
Thinking About Motivation
Purposeful Evaluation

In the context of the chapter they outline planning and learning activities of the committee; in that of in-service education they outline essential steps required to establish a learning environment, realistic expectations, and an awareness of change and growth.

CHAPTER 5

PLANNING SEQUENCE II: DEFINING THE PROBLEM AND IDENTIFYING RESOURCES

Probably no other aspect of in-service education has been written about or discussed as widely as needs assessment. Such data are, of course, the foundation blocks on which the program is to be built. No hunch, insight, or intuition of any one individual can be a reliable substitute. Although the data generated by a needs assessment often tend to be fragmentary and diversified, they do not have to be so. A comparison can be made to the highly selected materials that make up the elements of a foundation rather than to the carefully engineered foundation itself.

With a wealth of literature available on this subject, however, and with many teachers reporting that the unanswered questions of planning do not appear until after a needs assessment has been completed, the assumption will be made here that the committee of a dozen individuals introduced in chapter 4 has before it the results of a needs assessment conducted under the auspices of the central committee, the data have been analyzed and tabulated, and intelligent decisions have been made about which faculty groups to include in the current year's training program.

As it begins work on the second major planning elements, the committee's first task is to review the needs assessment data and, from them, to build the foundation stone of planning—a problem statement. This is to be followed by a thorough preview of the products to be ordered.

The agenda for the second component of the planning function, then, would consist of the following items:

1. Review of needs assessment data
2. Writing a problem statement
3. Previewing training materials.

REVIEWING THE NEEDS ASSESSMENT DATA

The presentation of the needs assessment data, organized in the best way possible, is the responsibility of the representative (or representatives) of the district committee selected to meet with the program committee. Distribution of this information would be the first item of business when the committee comes together for its second day of work. After reviewing the information, the committee's responsibility is to write a "problem statement" describing the specific problem addressed by the needs assessment and the expected outcomes of training. The problem statement will become the principal vehicle for communicating the goals and purpose of the program being planned to the teachers who will participate.

WRITING A PROBLEM STATEMENT

The following description of a problem statement was written by Anna Hyer, Research Director for the NEA study on the use of R&D products in in-service education.

If you walked into a store and said to the clerk, "I need a dress," you have stated a need or a problem, but you could not select a dress or enable the clerk to be of much help to you until you became much more specific.

Do you want the dress to wear to a wedding or to work in an office, or to pack for a trip to Europe? Do you want a dress that can be drycleaned or are you interested in drip-dry? Must the color scheme be one that will match accessories that you already have, or are you willing to buy new accessories if you like the garment? Do you want a dress that costs less than $50, less than $100, or less than $150?

These are some of the questions that you and the clerk will need to know before you can select an appropriate garment. "I need a dress" is a problem or need, but "I am interested in buying a dress for use in the summer for work in an air-conditioned office, one that is machine washable and that will require no ironing, in a color that will match white and/or blue accessories and that costs less than $50" approximates what is meant by a problem statement.

Of course, while you are in the store buying a dress meeting the specifications just listed, you may see another that is suitable for a tea dance, costing $100, dryclean only, and requiring completely new accessories. It has so much appeal that you decide to revise your statement of the problem and opt for meeting the new specifications rather than those originally set forth. This is called "recycling the problem."

If the same process is applied to in-service education, it can be seen that motivation and teaching math concepts or slow learners are broad general statements of need—not specific problem statements. Given the problem "teaching math concepts," both of the following statements might be developed by a client group.

Problem I. The math staff of a high school has insufficient time to adequately tutor students who need additional assistance for achieving in algebra and geometry. The staff has read about the use of computers in instruction, and the school has a computer on which time is available. However, only one member of the math department is familiar with the operation of computers. The math staff would like to learn enough about hardware and software functions of the school's computer so that they can develop programs to tutor the students having difficulty in algebra and geometry. The computer-assisted program is to follow the instructional sections outlined in the textbook.

Problem II. Many students at this K-6 school are not achieving math skills at a level of which they are capable. Among the reasons for this problem are the high rate of student ability from school to school during the year, and a widespread difference in student achievement levels in any one grade. As an approach to overcoming the problem, the teachers have developed a cumulative math card which records each child's progress in math skills. They expect to use this approach in teaching math on a more individualized basis, and they want to devise monthly in-service workshops to assist them in achieving their goal.

In other words, a need or problem is not the same as a problem statement. The former tends to be broad and general in nature, usually directly identified by teachers through a wide-ranging needs assessment. The problem statement is more detailed and specific and can be written either by the teacher to be served in the program or by the committee in charge of planning a specific in-service education activity.

There is no one right way to write a problem statement. The task is to strive for clarity and completeness. The more that can be stated about the reasons a problem is thought to exist, the greater the stated understanding of the conditions that will be changed once a solution is reached, the better the problem statement can be considered. In writing the statement try to include the following:

1.   What is the problem area?
2.   Why does it exist?
3.   Who are the intended participants? Who are the people affected?
4.   What, hopefully, will be different as a result of work on the problem?

Ideally, the teachers to be directly involved in the in-service program should write the problem statement. When this degree of direct democracy is impossible and a planning committee reviews the needs assessment data, a heavy burden of responsibility falls on the teacher members of that group. The committee members must be as careful as possible to speak for their colleagues, not for themselves. Before the third meeting of the committee, every effort should be made to distribute copies of the problem statement to teachers who will be participating in the program and to encourage their comment.

The actual mechanics of writing a problem statement from needs assessment data include the following steps:

1.   Select a recorder who will be responsible for filling out a newsprint (or chalkboard) outline summarizing the committee's discussion.

2.   Give each committee member a copy of the needs assessment data as organized and analyzed by the central committee. Allocate ample time for reading and comment.

3.   As a group, review the needs assessment data. In order to generate discussion, the chairperson might ask the following questions: "How are these data reflected in student and/or classroom behaviors?" "How long have these problems been around?" "What seems to be some of the causes of these problems?"

4.   After discussion, work toward a group consensus in formulating each part of a concise problem statement. Use the Reporter's Record (see Example 5) as a guide.

5.   Rework the items on the outline into a problem statement to be duplicated and submitted to all potential participants for their advice and comment.

Example 5. Problem Statement Outline

PROBLEM STATEMENT OUTLINE
(Reporter's Record)

1. The problem area:

    Subproblems:

2. Why the problem exists:

3. Characteristics of the intended participants (What do they have in common? How do they differ? How are they affected? Generalizations about their teaching experience and background):

4. What should be different as a result of work on the problem?

PREVIEWING TRAINING MATERIALS

Once the problem has been identified, a match must be made between the problem and products that offer hope of assistance. When previewing products, therefore, it is helpful for the planning committee to have in mind a set of criteria against which their usefulness can be judged. Matching on a continuum the characteristics of the product with those of the intended users, the human and time resources of the planning committee, and the support services of the district, represents one way of assessing the possible "fit." Figure 2 illustrates this approach.

Finding a correct "fit" between product and need is, of course, the crucial decision that must be made in product selection. There are, of course, other consideration such as those which follow.

1. Preview all products, especially films, filmstrips, audiotapes, and videotapes. In these materials the message remains locked up and out of sight until matched with the proper equipment for releasing it.
2. Review enough material to obtain a good idea of the overall product (not necessarily every component).
3. Check to make certain all the components are present. If they are not, contact the distributor immediately.
4. Carefully list all resource materials that accompany the products, and those that may be additionally required (either material or human, such as the group leader or facilitator).
5. Use the charts in Figure 2 (Matching Training Materials and Users) to help decide which products to order. Are the goals and objectives of the program compatible with those of the product? Is there enough similarity between the two to make a cohesive program? Is the theory being addressed in the product capable of the kinds of interpretation required to make it practical for implementation in the school environment?

Depending on program needs, additional considerations will suggest themselves. Preview time can also be used to begin to stimulate the imagination and to think about in-service education exercises that will lead toward a new and exciting learning for teachers relevant to their needs.

So many variables are involved in product selection that it is impossible to provide a general estimate of the time required. For purposes of the hypothetical committee mentioned earlier, it is assumed that a full half-day of the time set aside for the second segment of the planning committee will be used for previewing.

A few members of the committee, particularly those representing the central committee, may have reviewed the information on available resources that resulted in placing an order. Copies of the product descriptions used as a basis for selection and the Product Review Worksheet (see Example 8 in Chapter 9) should be on hand for committee reference.

It may not be necessary for every member of the planning committee to leave this session as an authority on every product. Whatever procedure is used to familiarize members with some or all of the selected products on hand, however, before going on to the next agenda item it is important that at least one committee member be well acquainted with at least one product available for potential use.

Figure 2. Matching Training Materials and Users

I. EXPERIENCE LEVEL OF GROUP EXPRESSING NEED; TEACHING STYLE OF PRODUCT

	1	2	3	4	5
Client group:	Extensive background in problem area. Need advanced materials. Interested in theoretical background.				A newly experienced problem area (i.e., students only now being mainstreamed in the classes of this group of teachers). See immediate applicability.
Product:	Postgraduate level. For use by experienced teachers.				Pre-service level. Emphasizes technique or ready-to-apply instructional hints.

II. TRAINING RESOURCES AVAILABLE; COMPLETENESS OF PRODUCT

	1	2	3	4	5
Support services available to client group:	Group leader (or training facilitator) available to organize program and secure resource material.				On their own. No outside help available.
Product:	Provides only an outline of a validated program. Lists resource materials that need to be secured.				Complete training package. Substantive presentations included on film or tape, pre- and post-tests, study guides, timetable of when to do what.

Figure 2. Matching Training Materials and Users (*continued*)

III. "MATCH" OF THE PRODUCT TO THE "NEED"

	1	2	3	4	5
Need:	Very precise; finely focused.				Highly generalized, covers "macro" rather than "micro" skills.
Product:	Deals with specific problem(s): outlines clear and exact procedures; specific techniques.				Theoretical in nature, suggests: broad methodology for problem solving.

IV. ADAPTATION POTENTIAL

	1	2	3	4	5
Planning Committee:	Has been given time to plan. Has members who are imaginative and inventive in their own teaching.				Time and/or imagination in short supply.
Product:	Is loosely enough designed that it can be used in part or in full (i.e., can be adapted to intermediate level even if advertised for secondary level).				Must be used as is. No room for adaptation.

Figure 2. Matching Training Materials and Users (*continued*)

V. MEDIA REQUIREMENTS

	1	2	3	4	5
Support services available:	Full range of media equipment available.				Equipment limited or unavailable.
Product:	Requires wide range of audiovisual equipment.				Uses print only.

VI. COST FACTORS

	1	2	3	4	5
Budget:	District has not budgeted funds for staff development of instructional personnel.				Professional development is a line item in the district's budget and the amounts allocated for a specific program are known to the planning committee.
Product:	Available at no cost through intermediate school district or by other means.				Will use all or a substantial portion of the allocated budget.

40

Figure 2. Matching Training Materials and Users (*continued*)

VII. GROUP SIZE

	1	2	3	4	5
Client group:	Large number of participants but "break-out" rooms available for subgrouping.				Few participants and/or some individual study programs.
Product:	Designed for large group presentations (i.e., film showings) and opportunities for subgroups.				Designed for (or easily adapted to) use by small groups or an individual.

VIII. EVALUATION

	1	2	3	4	5
Client group:	No need for evaluation. Participants sufficiently experienced to assess their own learning on their own responsibility.				Specific means of evaluation required either for "self-evaluation" or for instructor or group leader to use in certifying salary or academic credit.
Product:	Evaluation not addressed.				Complete guide to evaluating learning experiences provided.

41

THE TEACHER LEADER

Whatever the plan, whatever the goal, the increasing availability of new resources can be of great value to the program. The use of most products can be further enhanced if resource personnel, other teachers or members of the school staff are available to fulfill various leadership functions. Some products stand alone. Some must be combined with others or used simply as an outline for planning by an authorized committee. All lend themselves to creative, imaginative adaptation by a committee seriously seeking to fashion a program tailormade for the needs of the teachers it directly represents.

Many products call for a teacher-leader to assume organizational and group maintenance activities such as the following:

1. Making certain meeting facilities are available, products ordered, (and returned, if on loan), notices sent out, necessary records maintained. . .

2. Serving as a group leader at each session: helping to get discussion started, organizing and scheduling reports or small group activities, assisting members of the group plan the next session, facilitating whatever evaluation procedures are agreed upon. . .

3. Arranging for duplicating services for schedules, bibliographies, assignments, evaluation forms. . .

4. Arranging for, and then checking on, delivery to the in-service education site of any needed audiovisual equipment—and hopefully personnel for its operation.

5. Helping to secure access to a professional teachers' library or to an interloan library service for the purpose of securing needed professional materials.

6. Making arrangements to contact, and then brief, consultants or specialists brought in to the program.

These numerous support functions may be performed by a single person, often a teacher who may be asked to provide the services and be paid an appropriate honorarium. In larger school systems the office of the director of professional development sometimes has access to personnel whose duty is to serve the in-service education program. In some cases the principal and his or her office staff can make the necessary arrangements.

USING CONSULTANTS

The individuals who find themselves members of an in-service education advisory committee are usually selected for reasons other than their demonstrated skill in designing teacher training experiences. Teachers are selected because they are in a position to interpret teacher needs. Administrators and supervisors are selected because of their responsibility to understand, reflect, and monitor school board policy; their ability to command and channel into in-service education the necessary human and material resources; and their overall understanding of the skills required on the part of all personnel to meet the demands of the community for quality education.

The fact that probably none of the committee members are experts in in-service program design is not surprising. Such expertise is not a generally expected part of their background. Yet it must be present. Although methodological expertise is built in when an in-service education program is constructed around products, when product adaptation takes place, some additional familiarity with the design of learning experiences must be supplied by the local committee.

Similarly, content expertise may be lacking within the committee's membership. Again, this is to be expected. Individuals who have a subject mastery are not necessarily ideally equipped to plan a program. They can best serve as consultants or substantive experts at the times and in the order their contribution is considered most relevant by the committee.

In using products, the substantive *what* is built in along with the methodological *how*. When adapting products, particularly when extending them, content experts are often required to fill in gaps or to help relate one body of knowledge to another.

The NEA/NIE in-service education study observed that these two different kinds of expertise were frequently confused. When participating sites found it necessary to call in consultants for assistance in adapting products or designing pre- or post-exercises relating in-service learnings to direct classroom application, they were frequently disappointed. The consultants, usually curriculum people, tended to move immediately to substantive considerations—the "sequence and scope" of subject matter—and to leave unaddressed the questions of how, when, and under what circumstances teachers could learn more about teaching—i.e., the methodology of in-service education.

The study also gave evidence, however, that when planning committees *took the time* first to spell out for themselves the kind of assistance they needed and then to talk to potential consultants about such requirements, it was possible to find individuals who could meet exacting specifications.

CHAPTER 6

PLANNING SEQUENCE III: PROGRAM DESIGN

The heart of the in-service education program is the arrangement in logical, or perhaps pyschological, and cumulative sequence of the many learning strategies that comprise a total working design: lecture (whether in person or on tape or film), discussion, subgroup meetings, simulations, direct classroom application, individual projects, field trips, classroom observation. The detailed description of these strategies and their placement make the in-service education validated programs an extremely valuable tool.

If a given product turns out to be a semester-long, self-administering program of recorded lectures and films; if it has built in all the necessary ingredients—evaluation, classroom-oriented observation, and discussion topics; and if it matches the program time frame, the planning task is all but done. The organizing has already been done by someone else, and probably quite expertly.

On some occasions, however, the in-service activity may extend over a longer period of time than that for which the materials were planned and several products must be linked together to fully meet the needs expressed by the teachers. On other occasions the committee may find the resources at hand useful but requiring modification. (For example, an in-service education product on motivational skills addressed to middle school situation requires adaptation to meet the problems facing secondary school teachers.)

A quadruple task therefore confronts the planning committee in the beginning stages of program design:

1. Identifying learning strategies appropriate to the need to be met and the time available for in-service

2. Searching available program materials to uncover a useful range and variety of in-service education strategies

3. Inventing new strategies when the materials at hand fail to supply what is required

4. Adapting, revising, and arranging learning strategies into a workable sequence.

Designing an in-service education experience that matches the potential of the products to the needs expressed by the teachers thus becomes the major responsibility of the planning committee. One way for the committee to approach this bottom line of all in-service education planning—creating a training design—is to go back to the chalkboard or the newsprint as an aid to organize thinking.

A possible structure is suggested by Chart 1 which follows. Columns (a) and (b) on the chart represent a transfer of information and concepts developed earlier. The information required for columns (c) and (d) will be supplied as committee members report on the products that have been previewed for program consideration. Column (e) calls for a listing of the learning strategies which characterize the product: information giving, reality practice, observation, data collection, problem solving.

ARRANGING LEARNING SEQUENCES

Work on columns (f) and (g) often requires combining a willingness to go along with the learning strategies suggested in the products with a display of creative imagination by committee members in making adaptations.

Most products give detailed directions to a group leader on installing a wide variety of learning strategies. Frequently they supply audio and/or visual tools which have learning methodologies built into them. An example of the former would be directions for a role-playing situation spelled out in such detail that it is virtually fail-safe. It would provide briefing instructions for role participants and "what-to-watch-for" suggestions for the remaining members of the group. It would help the leader determine at what point to "cut" and provide a list of questions designed to encourage a full diagnosis of whatever slice of reality the episode was designed to replicate. Elements of even such a detailed example, however—the setting, the grade level, or the subject matter—can and should be modified by the planners if a modification will better fit a particular situation.

A pre-prepared learning tool might be a cassette tape which records an unresolved encounter between two students. How a teacher might deal with the situation is left for group discussion based on content material presented earlier.

Some products are designed to take learning into the teacher's classroom. They may outline games for a mathematics class and, in addition, provide a checksheet to help the teacher observe and note student reaction. Other products design large group learning activities for children that enable teachers to combine classes. They then go forward with suggestions to teachers on how to be supportive of each other—and to learn from each other—as they work together and observe each other.

Sometimes members of the planning committee are tempted to short-circuit the design. "Our teachers are looking for 'answers' to their problems—not games to play," they may say. Or "We don't have time for those fancy exercises"—interesting as they may be. Sometimes it is suggested that too many teachers will be participating in the in-service activity to make possible the execution of some of the learning exercises suggested.

The most tempting reason to avoid trying a new exercise may be the impulse to engage someone who "knows"—another teacher perhaps—to "tell" those who do not know. In some learning situations (reporting the results of an experiment, for example), this is more than adequate. In most situations the "telling," important as it is, profits from the additional opportunities to practice, to reflect, to critique, and to experiment. Such "internalization" of information— testing it and making it a part of behavior as well as a part of a knowledge base—contributes to lasting problem solving.

45

Chart 1. Product Utilization

A POSSIBLE STRUCTURE TO BE USED BY A PLANNING COMMITTEE

(a)	(b)	(c)	(d)	(e)	(f)	(g)	(h)	(i)
General needs	Specific problem to be solved (the problem statement—the client's goal)	Names of products that may help	Focus or scope of product (goal, substance, content, theme)	Strategies (methods, learning experiences, or exercises) employed by product	Adaptations required or desirable	Bright ideas on additional activities required to work on the problem statement. Give emphasis to in-classroom learning experiences.	Sequence in which training activities will be used (including pre- and post-workshop)	What new set of conditions is the use of this product, as adapted, expected to bring about?
1.	1.	1.	1.	1.	1.	1.		
2.	2.	2.	2.	2.	2.	2.		
3.	3.	3.	3.	3.	3.	3.		
4.								
5.								

ADAPTING TRAINING MATERIALS

Most replicable training programs, like most custom-made suits or dresses, require tailoring to assure a perfect fit. For successful adaptation, not only must the problems and characteristics of the client group be well known to the planning committee, but a considerable display of creativity may be in order. One of the most persistent adaptations required is changing the time frame from that proposed by a product to that permitted by the schedule. Some of these planning challenges are illustrated in Example 6.

AGENDA ITEM 3: INVENTING IN-SERVICE LEARNING EXPERIENCES

Sometimes the effort to make necessary adaptations, to design new learning strategies, results in a decision not to use any of the available products—but to create a new one—or, more exactly, to create an originally designed learning experience. In one community where the problem was helping teachers cope with "teacher stress," the planning committee was unable to find a suitable product. It elected therefore to draw upon known community resources it believed could assist in an examination of the medical, psychological, and physiological reasons for and treatment of stress. In advance consultation with the resource persons selected, the committee made every effort to guard against didactic presentations and to plan ways of addressing problems identified from the teachers' own experience.

On another occasion, learning experiences modeled on classroom occurrences were invented. For example, when teachers wished to learn more about the skills required to help students develop a classroom structure of their own, as a learning experience the teachers were deliberately placed in a nonstructured situation and, without outside help, were required to exercise their own initiative in building a workable structure. They were then asked to analyze the skills and attitudes needed to acquire this degree of self-government and self-discipline *for themselves*.

In another community, reviewing language arts products resulted in an instructional activity which used the newspaper as a learning tool. Among the techniques worked out by teachers in their in-service group were the following: identifying and cutting out letters in newspaper headlines that matched the letters of their own names for kindergarten children; writing the end of a story suggested by a comic strip for second grade children; and engaging in mathematics exercises built around comparison shopping for older students. Other teacher-developed activities included locating a job possibility through newspaper advertisements and writing a letter of application, "reading between the lines" in stories dealing with political or economic issues, finding story starters for English composition, and interpreting political cartoons.

Imaginative product adaptation, therefore, may result in, or grow into, results different from those initially visualized. If, in the process of adapting a product, teachers' needs are better met, if a richer learning experience results, then the committee can consider it has fulfilled its obligation to its clients.

Example 6. An Exercise in Product Adaptation

AN EXERCISE IN PRODUCT ADAPTATION: CHANGING THE TIME SPAN

On the pages that follow, descriptive information is provided about three products. Each of the products described was originally designed to cover a specific time span. Each one, however, may be adapted to a different time span.

This exercise is designed to help readers get the feel of product adaptation without actually previewing the components. This is an armchair exercise. It can be completed simply by reading the information provided and then sitting back and doing some imaginative thinking!

The assigned task is to take a product designed for one time span and adapt it to a longer time span. (The first two exercises may be completed on the basis of the information provided. The third is included for purposes of further illustration.) Here are a few starter ideas. Some of these suggestions for expanding the time frame may apply to all three products, others to only one or two. But as you work on the exercise, you will think of many more training ideas.

1. Consider the idea of a "reactor panel" of students (if age and maturity permit), of parents, of teachers from those included in the training group. Their role could be to serve as "reality testers" of whatever subject matter is presented by the product.

2. Explore the idea of having one member of the group "teach" in accordance with principles advanced in the product. One-half the members of the in-service group could then be assigned to serve as "students"; the others as observers.

3. Devise plans for the teachers in the in-service group to visit a class of one of the members of the group or of an acknowledged master teacher. Consider how much time should be allowed for some analysis of whatever teaching technique is demonstrated. Decide whether or not you would want the expanded design to include securing reactions from the students taught in the demonstration.

4. Invent a learning "game" which stimulates participant interaction in subgroups (for example: two or three teams participating in any combination of numbers compete to figure out the "best" strategy for coping with a particular problem).

5. Plan an assignment asking each participant to bring in an anecdotal account of student behavior for case analysis.

6. Arrange for subgroups within the training group to devise independent study products they wish to work on.

Note: Whatever suggestions for extending the learning sequence may occur, they should always be tested against the question "How does this help advance the learning outcome?"

Example 6. An Exercise in Product Adaptation *(continued)*

EXERCISE I.   EXPAND A PRODUCT DESIGNED FOR ONE DAY'S WORK INTO
A TWO-DAY WORKSHOP

Topic: Discipline

Name of Product: MULTIMEDIA MATERIALS ON DISCIPLINE

Publisher: National Education Association

Date: 1976   *Cost:* $68.67

The product includes four nine-minute audiotapes and two filmstrips
(each ten minutes). *Total time necessary to play/run these media and to
discuss them is six hours.* There are also three booklets and five pamphlets
(a total of 435 pages of printed matter). No time is suggested for reading
these resources. No instructions are given users for sequencing or adapting
these materials to an in-service education program. No evaluation of
teacher learning is enclosed.

Titles: DISCIPLINE: DAY BY DAY
(four audiocassettes: discussion questions for each)

DISCIPLINE TECHNIQUES
(filmstrip w/cassette narration, guide w/script and
questions)

CLASSROOM GROUP MANAGEMENT
(filmstrip w/cassette and leader's manual)

(Books and pamphlets: *Parents and Discipline, Behavior Modification,
Code of Student Rights and Responsibilities, Report of the Task Force on
Compulsory Education, Coping with Disruptive Behavior, Report of the
Task Force on Corporal Punishment, Discipline and Learning, Discipline
in the Classroom,* and *What Every Teacher Should Know About Student
Rights.*)

Training Outcomes: Twofold: To understand points of view among students, teachers,
administrators, and the general public about discipline, *and* to learn
techniques for dealing with discipline problems.

Adaptation Tasks: I.   Develop an outline for a two-day workshop based on the
materials available (assume reasonable running time of audio
and/or visual components) plus such other reinforcing or
supplementary activities as lend themselves to intensive
learning.

II.   Outline preparatory *and* reinforcement activities to precede and
follow the workshop. Give particular attention to classroom-
based activities in which the teacher can pinpoint needs and,
after the workshop, apply the knowledge and skills acquired.

49

Example 6. An Exercise in Product Adaptation *(continued)*

EXERCISE II: EXPAND A PRODUCT DESIGNED FOR A TWO-HOUR MEETING
INTO A FOUR-HOUR TRAINING SESSION

Topic: Educational Accountability

Name of Product: ALTERNATIVE AVENUES TO EDUCATIONAL
ACCOUNTABILITY

Publisher: Vimcet Associates, Los Angeles, California

Date: 1971   *Cost:* $20.00

The product includes a filmstrip and accompanying audiotape (listening
and viewing time comes to thirty minutes). The instructor's manual is four
pages long; it includes objectives, instructions for running tape/filmstrip,
and an examination. With discussion and testing the program comes to
about one hour.

Training Outcome: To expand the user's range of alternatives regarding the meaning of
educational accountability, i.e., the responsibility an educator is
supposed to assume for the quality of his/her efforts.

Adaptation Tasks: I.   Develop an outline of program activities to expand the
information/learning exercises in *Alternative Avenues to
Educational Accountability* from a two-hour meeting into a
four-hour training session.

II.   What reinforcement activities should follow the workshop? Give
particular attention to application potentials such as parent
groups, local association meetings, and faculty meetings.

EXERCISE III. EXPAND A PRODUCT DESIGNED FOR A TWO-WEEK COURSE
INTO A MONTH-LONG TRAINING PROGRAM

Topic: Special Education

Name of Product: A DECISION-MAKING MODEL FOR TEACHING THE
HANDICAPPED

Publisher: Center for Innovation in Teaching the Handicapped
Indiana University School of Education
Bloomington, Indiana

Date: 1974   *Cost:* $30.00

Example 6. An Exercise In Product Adaptation *(continued)*

Product includes a seventy-two-page instructor's manual, a ninety-three-page response book (for user), one cassette tape with filmstrip (ninety minutes). Time necessary for completion is two weeks. According to the developer it can be expanded to one semester. Evaluations are enclosed; a bibliography is listed.

Training Outcome: To increase the teacher's skill in using diagnostic assessment techniques when evaluating the instructional needs of exceptional children so that achievement-related prescriptions may be individually applied.

Adaptation Tasks: I.   Develop an outline of program activities to expand the information/learning exercises in *A Decision-Making Model for Teaching the Handicapped* from a two-week course into a month-long training program. Emphasize actual class contact (clinical learning).

II.   What plans for further training should be considered?

Note: Space does not permit providing enough information about the product to make it possible to complete this exercise. It is included as an additional example both to illustate the range of products available and to tempt speculation about the range of adaptation possible.

PROVIDING FOR PRE- AND POST-WORKSHOP LEARNING

When this point in program design is reached, half of the job is done. The first of the remaining tasks is to arrange the learning experiences—the activities recorded under columns (e), (f), and (g) on the Product Utilization Chart (given earlier in this chapter)—into a sequential pattern in column (h).

But when does a training activity begin—and end? In what setting does it get underway? How does the new learning keep on flowering?

To achieve and maintain maximum potential, the flow of training should be considered to begin before the first formal convening of teacher participants. Planning should also provide for learning to continue after the final group meeting. To help achieve such continuity, another simple chart, one divided into time segments, may help. Several different types are shown in Example 7. As the chart suggests, in-service education activities held at times when school is not in session (on weekends or during summer months) require that the committee plan for initial classroom-related teacher involvement in the program before the first formal meeting. Similarly, planning for classroom application of institute or workshop activities after the close of the final session is also indicated.

Activities planned to help bridge the transition from classroom to in-service course, workshop, or institute cannot be randomly selected. They must be considered an integral part of the workshop design. Fortunately, in planning most programs it is not necessary for the committee to invent pre- and post-training activities. Most products include suggestions of this kind. The pre- and post-test is very common. Sometimes the principal contribution of one product under consideration is to suggest learning situations that can be borrowed to provide a running start into the training program of another product.

Here are some examples of the kinds of classroom-related, pre-involvement activities that the product—or the members of the committee—might suggest.

1. Construct an assessment instrument to measure the entry level of background knowledge of each student into a new content area.

2. Write out a teaching guide to be followed with students at opposite ends of the classroom norm in the area to be addressed by the workshop. (What assistance is necessary? How should it be given?)

3. Observe how students react to various problem-solving or learning tasks if permitted to work in small groups.

4. Experiment with peer tutoring (for example, matching one student who reads well with another who verbalizes well). Ask students to suggest names of other students they think they would like to work with. Keep "before" and "after" achievement scores.

5. Identify a total unit of content to be taught. Chart two or three different teaching strategies that could lend themselves to this particular material: individualization, subgrouping, independent study, classroom interaction, teaching toward inquiry.

6. Arrange, when possible, for two teachers, or a small group of teachers, to begin work together before the in-service activity begins. Their assignment may be to gather data or make a list of projects in which they would like to work together. Teachers who are engaged in a similar or related teaching situation can serve as a sounding board for each other, ask questions to test the reality of proposed solutions, jointly plan to meet instructional problems, and provide each other with the wider range of knowledge and insight made possible by a differing set of teaching experiences.

USE OF THE CLASSROOM AS A LABORATORY

In advance of the in-service training activity, it is also important to consider post-training activities: learning activities related to the in-service content which can be continued in the teachers' own classrooms after the formal in-service education program has been completed. Once the use of validated in-service education products becomes familiar to participants, they can be used as part of a larger scheme—for building-level curriculum improvement, for example. More generally, precise planning for followup can take place once the in-service program gets underway and the participants themselves can begin to make their own plans for continued, systematic learning.

In a longer training program (see the ten-week example in Example 7), the pre- and post-training program, while desirable, does not have the same critical importance as in shorter programs. Here the planning committee's challenge is to devise methods for trainees, between meetings of the in-service group, to try out new learnings in the classrooms and then to report successes and failures to other trainees. When opportunities are provided for teachers to apply systematically and regularly in their own classrooms day by day and week by week the knowledge gained in the in-service education program, then the full potential of learning while teaching can be realized. Thus, the final session of a formally convened group learning experience, whether of short or long duration, should be a "commencement": a planning by each participant to put to use in a classroom situation at the earliest possible time what has been practiced, observed, listened to, and talked about in the training situation.

REVIEWING THE PLANNING COMMITTEE'S WORK

The final task of the planning committee is to check its own work. Some questions that may be helpful include the following:

1. Did we control the products (i.e., use them as tools in achieving our aim) or did the products control the planning?

2. Did we provide for a midpoint evaluation so that changes suggested by the participants, while the program was in progress, could be installed before the training was completed?

3. Did we give enough time and attention to structuring into the design methods whereby teachers could use their own classrooms as learning laboratories?

4. Did we think through well enough ahead of time the kinds of resource help we would need?

Example 7. Pre- and Post-Training Charts

WEEKEND WORKSHOP							
	Friday		Saturday		Sunday		
Pre- workshop activities		a.m. aft. eve.		a.m. aft. eve.			Post- workshop activities

SEMESTER
TEN-WEEK
2 OR 3 HOUR SESSION
EACH ONE WEEK APART

	1	2	3	4	5	6	7	8	9	10
1st hour										
2nd hour										
3rd hour										
Classroom- related activities										

SUMMER, TWO-WEEK INSTITUTE

	M	T	W	T	F			M	T	W	T	F	
Pre- institute activities						a.m. aft. eve.							Followup, wrapup, classroom related activities

5. Did we leave ourselves some flexibility in both time and money to make program or schedule changes should a midpoint evaluation make that seem desirable?

6. Did we—after finishing the planning, but before announcing the schedule—recheck the needs assessment data, the problem statement, and the available information about how teachers say they like to learn, to make certain we are doing what our clients want—not what we, the planning committee, seem to remember they want?

After the committee has completed its work on program design, a variety of administrative tasks remains. Responsibility for these tasks belongs to the central, districtwide committee and the district staff assigned to work with it. The administration of plans is as important as the creation of plans but does not necessarily require the time of the same individuals or the application of the same set of skills.

CHAPTER 7

INDIVIDUALIZING IN-SERVICE EDUCATION

Most frequently in-service education is considered in the context of a group activity: a class meeting after school, a circle of teachers tucked into a corner of the teacher center, or a handful of teachers from building A observing a colleague teach in building B.

When reviewing the options available for making in-service education as viable as possible, the joint teacher-administrator central policy committee should not overlook the possibility of officially installing in-service education as a systematically organized professional development program for individuals to pursue. There are teachers at the top of the salary scale who have no aspirations for further academic credentialing and no interest in enrolling in a class of any kind, who are nevertheless eager to learn more about the art and science of their own profession. They may not have an overriding "problem"; their interest is in learning more about teaching—and more about learning.

Other teachers, equally dedicated to the principle of learning for learning's sake, have the additional incentive of wanting to earn salary or academic credit. Even so, they are convinced that, within reasonable limits, they can learn alone just as productively as they can as a member of a class. For some teachers, an individualized approach to in-service education is an ideal response to a well-administered evaluation program. Self-study programs can be cooperatively designed to help a teacher with acknowledged skill gaps work through a course of studies developed to improve needed competencies.

INSTITUTIONALIZING SELF-INSTRUCTION

In the era of the districtwide, one-day in-service education institute, credit for participation in the event was frequently granted teachers who decided they had nothing to learn from the speeches or group sessions and could better spend time at their desks. A step above this in terms of acknowledging the importance of individual effort is the common practice of extending academic or professional credit to teachers who have completed individually organized travel or attended a professional conference. The same credit-granting arrangement lends itself to an independent course of study developed from validated in-service education materials. A manageable system would require an advance understanding that anticipated credit would be forthcoming after stated conditions were met. These might include the standard agreement on the relevancy of the problem statement and the goal outline explicit within; as well as the presentation of a paper, a teacher-made instructional product, or other evidence of personal growth, skill development, or deepened theoretical understanding at the end of the designated time.

Other institutional incentives and support systems for individualized in-service education include access to audiovisual equipment required for viewing and/or listening to product components and the opportunity to meet with other members of the school staff for individual consultation as the need arises.

The school administration can also help individuals with like interests find and maintain contact with each other. Teacher sharing has always been a favored method of learning, pairing a favored method of study.

Like the individual who elects to learn in concert with others, the teacher who embarks on an individualized program needs to be clear about ultimate goals. Random learning, like random dieting, while better than no effort at all, is no substitute for investing time in prior consultation, examining alternatives, and working out the details of a systematic plan of action.

The starting point for individualizing in-service education is the same as that for a group. It begins with the problem statement based on "needs" which can be drawn up by a teacher working alone or in conference with the principal or other instructional leader. In most cases, the analytical assessment of needs included in the problem statement can be furthered if there is an opportunity for interaction with another teacher, particularly one faced with a somewhat similar situation.

IN-SERVICE PRODUCTS AS THE VEHICLE

Many in-service education products and packages are ideally suited for individual use. Usually the "suggested activities" built into most products are designed for individual or small group use. They outline teaching techniques, observation schedules, interview guides, or student measuring devices that direct the teacher back into the classroom. These "laboratory excursions" may be designed as preparation for a new unit of content or as an application exercise. In either event, adaptation to individual use is often readymade.

Well-planned products bring an additional value to the individualized program. Part of the development process has been to work out a cognitive sequence which, sometimes logically—sometimes psychologically—leads through a series of learning experiences in an orderly progression from what is known to what is yet to be learned. Random experimentation with "what comes next" or the working out of an untried sequence can thus be avoided.

While most products have high adaptability for individual use, one state has prepared products specifically for individual use. In Ohio the Division of Educational Redesign and Renewal of the Department of Public Instruction has designed a series of in-service publications which give concise information about teaching methodologies and suggestions for application designed for use either in independent study or in working with a colleague. Further information may be obtained from the director of the division (Ohio Department of Public Instruction, 65 Front Street, Columbus, Ohio 43215).

A highly practical reason for using in-service education products as the foundation for programs of self-study is their capacity for reuse. After the activity has been completed, the products purchased for a program can be placed in the teachers' corner of the library or faculty lounge and made available to other educators. The consumable materials, almost without exception, can be purchased separately.

SOME DISADVANTAGES

Some individuals have successfully taught themselves to play the piano or learned a foreign language on their own. Others require the discipline of regularly scheduled lessons and study assignments. For those in the latter group, the explanation is doubtless more complex than slow motivation. Many factors condition the predictable success of a systematically organized program of individualized learning. They include the value placed by each individual on his/her own need for social interaction; established habits of initiative and perseverance; and the environment that exists at home or school for concentrated work.

A program of individualized study reduces the opportunity to learn from other students. In addition to the simple sharing of experiences, the generation of new knowledge and new insights that arise out of intellectual interaction will also be missed. Individual reflection does not of course preclude knowledge generation or insight development. It is reasonable to suppose, however, that even if the individual at the other end of the log, or conference table, is not Mark Hopkins, the insights developed on one's own can be deepened in dialogue with a studious colleague.

From an administrative point of view, monitoring progress is more difficult, or at least more time-consuming. For the individual student, self-evaluation is more subjective—harsher perhaps, more lenient perhaps—than if carried out in the midst of one's peers.

AND SOME ADVANTAGES

Individually planned in-service education can represent the ultimate in teacher needs assessment. No matter how finely tuned the need, if the necessary supports and services are brought into play, that need can be met.

Individual study places the student in competition with him/herself. Again, values and personal dynamics must be considered. In a group-oriented in-service program the highly competitive teacher may welcome this kind of setting as a stimulus for achievement. The more interdependent personality may equally welcome the group as a setting in which to help others and to learn from others. The individual influenced most strongly by highly personalized benchmarks of personal development, however, may perhaps grow best in an environment free from competition.

Individually designed in-service programs provide the teacher with the opportunity to progress at his/her own pace. With the crush of commitments pressing in on every teacher every day, the opportunity to tailormake learning to one's own schedule may be the greatest advantage of all.

In the NEA/NIE study of in-service education, only one state of the twelve participating in the pilot program provided an individual approach. The experience of that state suggests that individual programming of professional development deserves further experimentation. While a cost analysis directed at these comparisons was not a part of the study, it is possible that carefully organized, self-instructing products may represent a way for maximizing individual teacher involvement without corresponding increases in cost either to the teacher or to the district.

CHAPTER 8

NEW RESOURCES FOR IN-SERVICE EDUCATION

In the United States there are more than 16,000 school districts. Some have fewer than ten teachers. Some have more than 50,000. Some districts draw on great taxable wealth to support the educational program. Some are very poor. Some districts have extensive in-service education programs. More have none.

Every teacher in every district deserves an equal opportunity to increase individual competency. Teachers should not have to pay out-of-pocket to learn how to teach better. Neither should they always be expected to learn about teaching outside the classroom. There is no more practical way for teachers to learn about teaching than while teaching.

How can all this come about—in 16,000 different school districts? If experts-in-the-flesh are required to make an in-service education program work, there are not enough experts around. Even if there were, there is insufficient money to pay all of them. The need exists, then, to find practical ways to design and deliver a program that makes sense to teachers and whose cost does not make administrators wince.

One response to this need is through the use of the programs that have developed as a result of research into some aspect of in-service education. Many "products" of validated research are available for a relatively small cost. They may take the form of films, discussion outlines, multimedia packages, organizational plans for semester-long in-service programs built around a specified set of skills, training manuals, or any combination of these materials. (See Figure 3.)

THE IN-SERVICE EDUCATION PACKAGE

The opportunity to select, order, and use the products of educational research and development can be a rewarding experience. On some occasions it is comparable to looking over a roster of leading educational scientists and then selecting those to invite as consultants into your school or teacher center. If Eva Baker, James Popham, Ned Flanders, and William Glasser; Madeline Hunter or Beatrice Ward could attend in person, that would be an ultimate experience. But when funds and schedules make that impossible it is nearly as rewarding, through the magic of the motion picture, to hear and see them lecture or—as is sometimes the case—to watch children engage in learning activities under their supervision. In some products, the motion picture is replaced by taped lecture, interview, or dramatized problem situations. Other products may resemble a textbook with a series of learning activities appended to each section.

In its simplest form the product may be no more than a large envelope containing an outline of books—or chapters—to be read, a discussion outline of issues and problems raised in the reading, observation schedules to use in watching various aspects of classroom learning, and ideas for teachers to consider in evaluating their own learning.

In its most complete form, the package would be literally that: a box containing recorded lectures accompanied by films that demonstrate the application of theoretical material, as well as all the ingredients for evaluation, classroom-oriented observation, and group discussion topics that have been previously used and worked out in ongoing programs.

Figure 3. Illustration of a "Product"

Thus, far from short-circuiting the expertise found in institutions of teacher training and specialized research, the use of prepared materials provides a practical, efficient way to funnel the results of research, much of which originated in colleges and universities, directly to a school faculty.

Detailed information and directions for finding
and ordering in-service education materials
appear in Chapter 9
Locating and Ordering the New Resources

THE NEED FOR PLANNING

The simple availability of products, however, does not mean that teachers and administrators no longer have an obligation to carefully plan the activities of teacher centers or in-service education programs. Quite the opposite is the case.

As has been noted, products come in all shapes, sizes, and degree of complexity or completeness. Even with the most comprehensive—those which, in a single package, spell out a full range of learning experiences from "introducing the idea" through "evaluating what we have learned"—as much careful planning is required for effective use as if a visiting lecturer were scheduled to present a course or a teacher were asked to prepare a teaching demonstration.

When anticipating use of a number of books, films, outlines, or cassettes, related only by virtue of common subject matter, effective planning becomes even more difficult. Planning to use and relate these materials is a specialized skill and, although it builds on other, more familiar skills, it represents a unique art form.

COST EFFECTIVENESS

As with everything else, the cost of available products varies. Some materials which consist of an outline of books, discussion guides, and observation schedules are very inexpensive. Multimedia packages—a combination of filmstrips, motion picture films, books, and videotapes—are more expensive. Often there are options to consider when selecting a multimedia package—for example, it may not be necessary to order all components and this reduces the cost. Pricing information is usually a part of any product description.

The NEA In-Service Education Project found that the average cost of the product selected by project sites to be used in an in-service education program was $60. Thus it would seem that in addition to other advantages, the use of already-developed training materials has the potential of bringing the basic tools of in-service education within the reach of *every* school district. The products ranged in price from $0.25 to $2,165. The median cost was about $28. The least expensive items are outlines listing resource materials used and in-service training programs that worked. The most expensive items are complete training programs made up of many different components. All are capable of almost limitless reuse.

CHAPTER 9

LOCATING AND ORDERING THE NEW RESOURCES

The abilities to retrieve information about educational materials and then to demonstrate the expertise required to secure them as promptly and economically as possible are specialized skills. Individuals possessing these skills are usually employed within a local school system or on call from one of its support systems such as an intermediate school district or equivalent. As a result of graduate study or other professional preparation, many teachers have an extensive background in in-service education products.

After the first step, the needs assessment, has been completed, the analysis will usually reveal a wide spectrum of possible areas for in-service education—particularly if a large number of teachers are involved. Information about available training programs must then be found. If preliminary investigation indicates that the programs identified will meet an expressed need, then an order must be placed for their rental or purchase.

To help facilitate the search for usable materials, the NEA project selected 132 of the 650 R&D-based in-service products it had described and prepared an *Annotated Bibliography* (available from ERIC) which gives a brief description, grade level, developer, distributor, and cost.

Also available from ERIC is descriptive information about each of these 132 products in a seven- or eight-page format. The first page, Summary Information, is a brief review of the product's characteristics. Pages two through six provide in-depth information about the products, including purposes, content, activities, and resources involved in use of the product, ordering information, and history of development. The seventh page, Describer Critique, gives the evaluative comments of the person who has described the product. When included, the eighth page, User Critique, reports the reactions of teacher users.

USING ERIC

How can these product descriptions be found? By searching the materials of the *Education Resources Information Center* (ERIC), an information collection and dissemination service supported by the National Institute of Education. Many school systems, intermediate service agencies, schools of education, and state departments of education subscribe to the monthly ERIC indexes, *Resources in Education* (RIE), and *Current Index to Journals in Education* (CIJE), and to the ERIC Microfiche Collection of RIE Documents. CIJE announces journal articles appearing in more than 700 education-related journals. RIE announces and provides access to educational documents, including research descriptions, conference proceeding instructional materials, and product descriptions of the 132 sets of materials listed in the *Annotated Bibliography*. The *Annotated Bibliography* itself is also listed in ERIC.

Most of the RIE documents, including the product descriptions, are available in microfiche from those sites subscribing to the ERIC Microfiche Collection. A "microfiche" is a four-inch by six-inch piece of film that stores up to ninety-five full pages of print, each reduced to the size of a fingernail. A machine called a "reader" is used to magnify the image on the small film to full size for reading. A "reader/printer" performs as both a reader and a photocopy of any given page.

If one wished to find the descriptive information about one of the 132 products listed in the *Annotated Bibliography*—for example, *Parents as Partners in Teaching Handicapped Children*—how would that particular microfiche be located out of the approximately 165,000 that now make up the ERIC Microfiche Collection?

One place to start the search is RIE, which has listings in each edition by subject, author, and institutional source. Checking under subject headings ("descriptors") such as In-Service Teacher Education, Parent Participation, Handicapped Students, or under the National Education Association, Project on Utilization of In-Service Education R&D Outcomes in the Institutional Source Index would be appropriate. Each listing includes an accession number—preceded by ED—that leads to both the document abstract in the front of RIE and to the microfiche being sought.

Another ERIC tool to consult is the ERIC *Title Index*, listing RIE document titles alphabetically, and providing the accession number to the right of the title. For the preceding example, ED 164 539 would be located and would lead directly to the microfiche collection. Once the document is located, it can be read on the reader or reader/printer.

New, validated in-service education programs, a variety of documents and journal articles about in-service teacher education, and other products are developed and published every year. Many of these will find their way into ERIC. Descriptors—the subject headings used in RIE nd CIJE—provide the key to locating these materials. The complete listing of ERIC descriptors may be found in the *Thesaurus of ERIC Descriptors*.

The following descriptors should be of help in finding additional information in ERIC: In-Service Teacher Education, Instructional Materials, Learning Modules, Programmed Materials, specified subjects (e.g., reading, social studies).

For further information on searching ERIC indexes, or for the address of a nearby site subscribing to the ERIC products, contact the ERIC Clearinghouse on Teacher Education, One Dupont Circle, NW, Suite 616, Washington, D.C. 20036 (202) 293-7280.

PUBLISHERS' CATALOGS

The catalogs of commercial publishers are also a useful source of information. In most schools they will be found in the professional library, the purchasing department, or the offices of the various subject matter supervisors. It is always possible to write directly to the publishers for individual copies. (Use the address found in the advertisements in the professional journals.) Most of the materials advertised will be instructional items for use with children since this is, by far, the largest market. In-service education materials, however, are usually listed under a separate heading.

HELP IN LOCATING PRODUCTS

Before any teacher undertakes an independent search for products, it is usually helpful to check first with others in the school system—librarians, media specialists, department heads, curriculum personnel—who may already have access to information of the kind just suggested. Often personnel in the state department of education can be of assistance. Finding a way of reaching into that maze of bureaus and departments may not be as difficult as might be expected. In most cases a letter addressed as generally as "Supervisor of (for example) Foreign Language Instruction, State Department of Education, State Capitol Building" will be routed to the right person. Individuals holding such positions usually have access to specialized lists that are not generally available. For example, various clearing-houses in the ERIC system distribute newsletters and product announcements to those on their mailing lists from time to time. These particular publications are announced in *Resources in Education* and are made available on microfiche.

The staff of college and university education departments may also be a prime source of help in seeking information on the availability of in-service education products.

If, after all these measures, there are still problems, teachers who are members of a professional association should call or write the state headquarters, telling them of their membership and the need for help in locating readymade in-service education materials in the specialty represented.

REVIEWING PRODUCT INFORMATION

The preceding steps do no more than turn up the names of products to choose from and provide a brief abstract of the contents. Such information may range from lengthy critical reviews by an authority in the field to a publisher's promotional paragraph. It could result in clippings, printouts of information displayed on the screen of an ERIC reader, or descriptive annotations in a subscription service such as that available from the Educational Products Information Exchange Institute.*

Locating and organizing into usable form information about in-service education materials is a job that requires the expenditure of time, under the best of circumstances. *Reviewing* the information uncovered by the search and reaching a decision as to which items to purchase, calls for the expenditure of still more time. *The final selection must be made by an individual or, preferably by a group of individuals, attuned to the subtleties of the needs assessment data and able to sense the appropriateness of a given product for a given purpose.*

In some situations an outline of an in-service education program costing as little as a quarter may be required. In others, a full set of self-administering training materials may be necessary. In most cases a combination of different kinds of training tools is needed.

---

*The Educational Products Information Exchange (EPIE) Institute is a nonprofit organization that provides educators with information and counsel, based on impartial and independent studies, on the availability, use, and effectiveness of educational materials, equipment, and systems. For further information, write the EPIE Institute, 475 Riverside Drive, New York City, New York 10027, or call (212) 870-2330.

Ideally, representatives from the target clientele, i.e., the teachers in a particular building or faculty group, should review product information and share in decision making about which ones to order. Reviewing a wide range of product descriptions frequently helps clarify and focus more closely on the areas of requested assistance expressed more generally in many needs assessments.

Involvement of the client group at this point may not always be feasible, however. For example, a highly effective source of information about potentially needed products is the evaluation data contributed by participants in an in-service program coming to a close at the end of the school year. Locating and ordering products to meet needs so identified becomes a task that lends itself to summertime work. When this is possible, the needed materials for the next sequence of training can be anticipated and will be available when school reconvenes in the fall.

However the information may be reviewed, the next step is deciding which materials to order, on the basis of the information available. An Educational Products Worksheet is helpful in reaching this decision. A suggested outline is provided in Example 8. Few product descriptions or publishers' announcements will supply all the information needed, but the worksheet may suggest some items that, if needed and not otherwise available, can be secured by sending an inquiry to the publisher or developer. If representatives of the client group cannot be included in the purchase selection process, copies of the Product Review Worksheet (Example 8) should be saved and made available to the members of the program planning committee when it meets to preview the products that will be at its disposal.

ORDERING PRODUCTS

When an order is placed, in-service education products are no different from other educational or instructional materials. In writing a purchase requisition it is well, however, for the individual from whose budget the purchase price will come to keep in mind the following:

Product rental. Many products can be rented for a period of up to one week. It is a good idea to check on rental policy when considering films and videotapes.

Discounts. Vendors do not usually volunteer an unpublished discount. However, materials which are ordered in quantity for widespread use in in-service programs or teacher centers may qualify for discounts. The discount varies depending on the distributor, quantity ordered, and sometimes a promotional consideration.

Thirty-day approval policy. The approval policy, when available, means that there is a thirty-day grace period before paying for the product. If the product does not meet program needs, it can be returned before thirty days and credit will be issued for the invoiced amount. The only bill received is for shipping and handling. Under certain circumstances this provides an opportunity to preview products, but care must be taken that if materials are returned they are in the same condition as received.

The person in the school system who regularly orders books and supplies will have had experience in ordering instructional materials and may be knowledgeable about securing the most favorable discounts. That person may also have at hand a bag of tricks to employ when delays in delivery, mixups in billing, or mistakes in pricing occur. Such expertise is an important part of the school district's support for the in-service education program.

Example 8. Product Review Worksheet

1. Product title: _____

   _____

2. Product description(s) read by: _____

3. Sources of information (check one or more):

   _____ ERIC description

   _____ Publisher's catalog

   _____ Other (specify) _____

4. Comparative information:

Part I What We Need	Part II What the Product Offers
Program goal: _____	Product Goal: _____
Leadership resources available: _____	Leadership resources required: _____
Equipment available: _____	Equipment required: _____
Funds available: _____	Cost of product: _____
Times available: _____ Level (beginning teachers, experienced teachers, etc.): _____	Time required: _____ Level: _____

5. Can product components be rented?   _____ Yes   _____ No

6. Can separate components be used or must product be used in its entirety?

   _____ Separate products

   _____ Entire product

7. Can product be used with other products?   _____ Yes   _____ No

8. Were teachers involved in its production?   _____ Yes   _____ No

66

CHAPTER 10

WHO DOES WHAT WHEN

In programs financed from local funds, only the school board can legally set policy. But in the still-emerging field of teacher-centered in-service education, definitive policy often does not exist. Successful practice makes policy. In at least one school district included in the NEA study, the operation of a demonstration program resulted in the participants drafting a policy statement on in-service education for presentation to the board of education.

The law authorizing the federal teacher centers provides that a majority of the members of the funded teacher center policy boards must be teachers. The remaining members may represent whatever other interests the writers of the proposals consider relevant to the purposes and structure of the center. In practice the remaining members generally represent one or more school jurisdictions, institutions of higher education, and various other groups broadly defined as "the public."

To further complicate sorting out who is planning what and who is doing what, a number of districts have still another set of in-service education programs—those authorized from funds secured by the district to support categorically aided programs. Title I, programs for the handicapped, bilingual/bicultural education, vocational education, and adult basic education are a few of the special areas enabled to secure funds for designated types of teacher in-service education training. Whenever possible, the coordination of these programs is an important responsibility of the districtwide, central in-service education committee.

In spite of all the activity taking place in some districts, in others talk about in-service education is more usual than action. When this is the case, if events reach the point that someone wants to do something about the situation, the many tasks awaiting attention tend to blur technical distinctions of who should do what. Who *can* do what becomes the basis of much decision making! Who—whether teacher or administrator—with an already heavy load is willing to take on an extra task?

PLANNING PRINCIPLES

As observed earlier, the whole field of in-service education is still taking shape and form. It is not surprising therefore that the governance and administrative patterns of in-service education are sometimes marked by complexity and confusion. Yet the design for teacher involvement in program planning remains relatively straightforward. This book has advanced four principles:

1. Central, districtwide policy formation

2. Highly decentralized program planning

3. Representation of both teachers and administrators on all levels—district and school and/or faculty

4. Faithful adherence to a systematic planning process.

No matter how many separate programs may be operating in a district—whether federally funded or locally supported—these planning principles remain the same. A federally funded training program for teachers of children who are not literate in English requires the same level of teacher involvement, the same use of a problem statement, and same attention to building or faculty-group decentralized planning as does a program arising out of a districtwide needs assessment or the deliberations of a teacher-center policy board.

For the central committee on top of one or more of these structures to plan in too much detail takes away from the participants the adventure of charting a course of action. "Overplanning"—even when by a committee of duly appointed teachers—can leave possible participants with the feeling that they have no control over their learning destiny. On the other hand, planning too loosely leaves the client groups adrift, prepared only to sail off in every direction. Finding the exact mix of *planning for, involving in,* or *delegating to* is perhaps the single most important—and difficult—task faced by any in-service education committee.

THE TEACHER CONSTITUENCY

Teachers are members of an in-service education program planning committee for a purpose: to articulate teacher needs and perceptions from a teacher's point of view. To do this adequately they need to be assured of the backing of their colleagues. In case of conflict or disagreement within the committee they should be able to turn to their colleagues to serve as a sounding board. The natural and logical linkage is with their local teachers association; more specifically with its executive committee or the subcommittee charged with looking after in-service education.

In terms of immediate support it is the responsibility of the local association to monitor in-service education activities in the district, to provide its representatives on planning committees with such clerical or office support as they require, and to insist through bargaining procedures or other means that enough time be devoted to planning, on school time, so that whatever programs are offered can fulfill their potential.

Teachers at the local, state, and national levels of their organizations must be involved in the support of in-service education in such tangible ways as influencing legislation, developing administrative regulations, and appropriating funds required to support and extend effective teacher-centered in-service education. To do so, the needs of the constituency must be regularly assessed, a position established, accurate and verifiable data collected, legislative assistance enlisted, and the support of effective allies recruited. Not to be overlooked is the importance of a fair degree of patience. The enactment of Section 532, "Teacher Centers," of the Education Amendments of 1976 demonstrates what can be done. Those who followed the long legislative history of this bill know that representatives of teacher organizations were an important and influential part of the legislative drive.

THE PUBLIC AS A CONSTITUENCY

Implicit within the concept of teachers and administrators jointly planning in-service education programs is the understanding that members of the school administrative staff represent the board of education and that members of the board of education represent and draw their power from either those members of the public who vote for them directly or those who appoint them.

Teachers understand that not all in-service education can be exclusively teacher-centered, that is, focused solely on teacher needs as teachers see them. Nor is it reasonable to think that all in-service education will always be delivered in a manner that serves pressing instructional needs of personnel in the classroom, library, counseling office, health center, or other teaching/learning environment.

An important obligation of the school administration and the board of education is to plan and offer programs designed to promote knowledge and proficiency of instruction in specific curriculum areas and to enable employees to meet the shifting demands of the total organization. From the standpoint of faculty motivation and learning, however, employee involvement in planning in-service education programs growing out of long-range policy or management plans is as important as that for programs growing out of classroom instructional needs.

JOINT RESPONSIBILITIES

Without violating responsibilities to their respective constituencies, the representatives of both the school administration and the teachers have numerous tasks in common. One of those tasks—cooperatively planning in-service education programs—has been the focus of this book. The emphasis on the use of R&D in-service products is, in a sense, incidental. In-service education materials of the kind described in this book are a convenient, accessible means of bringing expert knowledge about instructional questions to teachers everywhere at small expense.

Nor is the cooperative planning of in-service education programs for teachers the end of the responsibility of all members of the school staff to work together for school improvement. Projections about the purpose, methods and goals of in-service education have long been an almost-exclusive concern of state departments of education staff, the faculties of schools of education, and the curriculum personnel in local school districts. Their concern for, and their devotion to, this task must continue. But as teacher involvement in decision making about in-service education program planning continues to grow, so will teacher interest and concern in questions of finance and school organization as they relate to in-service education. Such an outcome is to the advantage of all. Program planning is inevitably tied to such issues as rearranging the school day in ways that will help teachers find time to learn from one another. It must concern itself with bringing academic resources into the school at times and under circumstances compatible with the teachers' own "teachable moments." These innovations will take time to design and money to implement.

Lack of money may not be the basic obstacle to change, however. Salary increment courses offered by the school district, sabbatical leave programs, in-service education "days," are costly. Most school districts already spend considerable funds on all or most of these activities. A more difficult problem may be squarely facing questions such as the following: Are courses and classes the only way to earn academic or salary credit, or are they the most administratively feasible way? Is the earning of academic credit and/or salary credit the most effective incentive for the career-long education of teachers? Can the structure of the school day be changed in ways that will free more hours for in-service education without interrupting the instructional program for students or incurring the costs of substitute pay? Can in-service education—the process of constantly becoming a better teacher—be a condition of work, an integral part of every teaching assignment? How can teachers be involved in planning not only the details of their own staff development but also in thinking through its purposes, its philosophy, its structure, and its setting?

The answers to these and similar questions will depend upon factors that vary from one local situation to another and from state to state. Teachers in one school district may attach a high priority to seeking a voice in the determination of policies governing their in-service program, while those in another school district may not. The managers of one school system may have historically courted full teacher involvement in instructional decision making, and quite the opposite situation may hold in a neighboring system. But, allowing for local variation, the process by which teachers and administrators can and do work together on these questions is becoming increasingly clear: it is the formal, collective agreement. This form of collaboration, a legally sanctioned decision-making relationship between teachers and the board of education, is the means by which members of the teaching profession can become involved with representatives of the public and the managers of the school system in working for change.

The preparatory school for this heady experience is the much-referred-to joint committee: teachers and administrators planning continuing learning experiences that serve teachers and thereby the public that employs them.

APPENDIX

PROJECT ON UTILIZATION OF IN-SERVICE EDUCATION R&D OUTCOMES
NATIONAL EDUCATION ASSOCIATION

STATE FACILITATORS

Alabama

Mary Colleen Taylor
Alabama Education Association
P.O. Box 4177
Montgomery 36101
(205) 834-9790

James O. Turnipseed
Coordinator of Departmental Teams
Alabama State Department of Education
Montgomery 36130
(205) 832-3263

California

John Bright
628 Cuesta Avenue
San Mateo 94003
(415) 341-4571

William E. Webster, Director
Office of Staff Development
California State Department of Education
721 Capitol Mall
Sacramento 95814
(916) 322-5537

Jim Williamson, Consultant
Instruction and Professional Development
California Teachers Association
1705 Murchison Drive
Burlingame 94010
(415) 697-1400

Iowa

Merrill D. Halter
Teacher Education and Certification
Iowa Department of Public Instruction
Grimes State Office Building
Des Moines 50319
(515) 281-3437

Richard L. Sweeney, Director
Instruction and Professional Development
Iowa State Education Association
4025 Tonawanda Drive
Des Moines 50312
(515) 279-9711

Massachusetts

Fred Andelman, Assistant Director
Professional Development Division
Massachusetts Teachers Association
20 Ashburton Place
Boston 02108
(617) 742-7950

Patricia Prendergast
Director of Teacher Education
North Adams State College
North Adams 01247
(413) 664-4511

Michigan

Charles King
Professional Development
Michigan Education Association
P.O. Box 673
East Lansing 48823
(517) 332-6551

Barbara Carlisle
Michigan State Department of Education
P.O. Box 30008
Lansing 48909
(517) 373-3608

Minnesota

Nancy Sinks, Assistant Director
Instruction and Professional Development
Minnesota Education Association
41 Sherburne Avenue
St. Paul 55103
(612) 227-9541

Ohio

Nancy Eberhart, Assistant Director
Division of Educational Redesign and Renewal
Ohio Department of Public Instruction
65 Front Street
Columbus 43215
(614) 466-2979

Edward F. Jirik, IPD Director
Ohio Education Association
225 East Broad Street
Columbus 43216
(614) 228-4526

Pennsylvania

Randall Bauer, Advisor
In-Service Education
Pennsylvania Department of Education
P.O. Box 511
Harrisburg 17126
(717) 783-1830

Bill Steinhart
Professional Development
Pennsylvania State Education Association
400 North Third Street
Harrisburg 17101
(717) 255-7000

Tennessee

H.B. McDonough
701 Vanoke Drive
Madison 37115

Washington

Wayne Hall
Washington Education Association
910 Fifth Avenue
Seattle 98104
(206) 622-1810

Alf Langland, Associate
Professional Development
Washington Department of Public Instruction
Olympia 98504
(206) 753-1031

Wisconsin

Robert Skeway, Consultant
Continuing In-Service Education
Bureau of Teacher Education and Certification
Wisconsin Department of Public Instruction
Madison 53603

Ed Gollnick, IPD Program Director
Wisconsin Education Association Council
101 West Beltline Highway
Madison 53713
(608) 255-2971

Wyoming

Donald W. Shanor, Executive Secretary
Wyoming Education Association
115 East 22nd Street
Cheyenne 82001
(307) 634-7991

Alan Wheeler, Director of Curriculum Services
Wyoming State Department of Education—Hathaway Building
Cheyenne 82002
(307) 777-7411